D1231792

1111 3   19.95

The Life
of
Franklin Pierce

Painting by Irvin E. Alleman of Franklin Pierce and Nathaniel Hawthorne visiting Rome in 1857. Used by arrangement with the National Geographic Society, © 1966.

The Life
of
Franklin Pierce

By Nathaniel Hawthorne

with additions by the
Students and Faculty of
Kenneth A. Brett School,
Tamworth, New Hampshire

Published for the Tamworth School District

by

Peter E. Randall Publisher
Portsmouth, New Hampshire
2000

45209/32

Published by the Tamworth School District
Tamworth, New Hampshire

Additional copies available from

Kenneth A. Brett School
881 Tamworth Street
Tamworth, New Hampshire 03886

Produced by
Peter E. Randall Publisher
Box 4726, Portsmouth, NH 03802

This is a new edition of Nathaniel Hawthorne's *Life of Franklin Pierce* originally published in Boston by Ticknor, Reed & Fields in 1852. The first edition
was 12,952 copies, with 52 destroyed as defective. Of these, 9,790 were in
wrappers (5,000 of these were distributed by the New York Democratic
Party) and 3,110 in various cloth bindings. Copies in wrappers are now
counted as one of the Hawthorne rarities, the vast majority of surviving
copies being in cloth.

Library of Congress Cataloging-in-Publication data

Hawthorne, Nathaniel, 1804-1864
   The life of Franklin Pierce / by Nathaniel Hawthorne : with additions by
the students and faculty of Kenneth A. Brett School, Tamworth, New
Hampshire.
    p.cm.
   ISBN 0-914339-93-1 (alk. paper)
   1. Pierce, Franklin, 1804-1869. 2. Presidents--United States--Biography.
I. Kenneth A. Brett School (Tamweorth N.H. : Town) II. Title.)
E432.H38 2000
973.6'6'092--dc21
   [B]
                                                        00-051715

CONTENTS

A painting of Franklin Pierce done late in his Presidency. Courtesy New Hampshire Historical Society (NHHS).

FOREWORD

The idea for this publication came as students enjoyed a class trip to Salem, Massachusetts. As our students visited the "House of the Seven Gables," inspiration for one of Nathaniel Hawthorne's greatest works, Brian Wiggin, who teaches social studies at the Kenneth A. Brett School, began to remember the close relationship Hawthorne shared with New Hampshire's only President, Franklin Pierce. Wiggin's early fascination with all things Presidential led him into politics on a statewide and national level and furnished him with a love of New Hampshire history. As a collector of old books, he wondered aloud to the curator of the "Gables" museum, "Why hasn't anyone republished the Hawthorne biography of Pierce? Everything else by the famous author seems to be in print." The Curator quipped "It's up to you people in New Hampshire to do that," with the insinuation that only New Hampshire citizenry could possibly be interested. That remark turned out to be the challenge that generated this new volume. Brian walked away thinking "Let's do it."

When Brian mentioned his idea to me it seemed like a natural winner. As a book collector and seller for many years, I was well aware of the passion elderly volumes could inspire in students and curious adults. As a School Media Specialist, I knew that completing the publication process would offer many opportunities for "real life" learning experiences for our students. Soon we decided to involve every student in our class of 32 eighth graders and to create a quality hard cover publication with the best material for illustrations we could find.

Our first challenge was to find a copy of the book that Hawthorne wrote in 1852, just a year after he wrote his famous *Seven Gables*. The biography Hawthorne wrote in 1852 was a far different work from the books tracing Puritanism that built his reputation as one of America's major authors. Hawthorne agreed to write a campaign biography for one of his best friends who suddenly and unexpectedly became a presidential candidate and described the effort as "remote from (my) customary occupations." Copies of Hawthorne's *Life of Franklin Pierce* are rare. We were able to obtain a photocopy of the original from the New Hampshire State Library. As I looked for information on Pierce it became obvious that there was little in print about the fourteenth president. Many of the scholarly works on Pierce from previous generations were sincerely disparaging. During the project we found mention of Pierce in a *Time* magazine article which described him as the "punching bag" of presidential history. We also encountered a review of a Y2K campaign biography in the *New York Times Book Review*, which suggested that Hawthorne's work on the Pierce biography demeaned the great artist and criticized *The Life of Franklin Pierce* as a "piece of hack work and gaseous flattery."

As teachers rather than political pundits we decided that we would offer students the opportunity to assess Pierce on their own. As teachers we were more skeptical than academic historians. Brian was aware that "There are so many things about Pierce that nobody knows." He was capable of reciting the facts. "He is the only president who memorized his inaugural speech. He is the only one who did not have to make even one cabinet change. He was aggressive in developing international trade. It was while he was president that Commodore Perry went to Japan. There are a lot of positive things that he did and he should not be at the bottom of the presidential pile." I knew it would be impossible to convince the nation to enshrine the fourteenth president in a comparison with Lincoln, Jefferson, or Washington, but I also knew that a hands-on study of Pierce would give our students a better understanding of the man and his times than any amount of exposure to the "conventional wisdom."

We started by developing a list of committees who would tackle the project. Each student chose which committee to join and which part of the task to accomplish. Almost all students worked on the process of comparing the photocopied original to an on-line version to make sure our edition of the book was true to the original. The process immersed the students in the language of 1852 as no other project could. Many of the words were archaic and had to be researched. The style was definitely pre-modern. To do the job they were obligated to study each word in the text just as if they were proofreading a composition for class. Instead of walking in Hawthorne's footsteps they were thinking in Hawthorne's sentences. When we had finished the task of rectifying the text, we began the process of choosing illustrations and designing the book.

We conducted field trips to the New Hampshire Historical Society Library, the Museum of New Hampshire History, the Pierce Manse in Concord, the Pierce Homestead in Hillsborough, and the Pierce Memorial in the North Main Street Cemetery. We were able to assemble a compelling and beautiful set of illustrations for the publication using these resources. We believe that combining an original primary resource on Pierce with the best illustrations our students could find will result in a valuable book. We know our edition will never be as valuable intrinsically as the rare first edition. Our goals were not intrinsic. We set out to teach respect for government and the office of the presidency and a critical thinking approach to history and social studies. We have been able to convince our students to assess the strengths and weakness of the fourteenth president, who has in turn been castigated and forgotten, and so we believe that our edition of the book is the more valuable.

John E. Perkins
Media Specialist
Kenneth A. Brett School, 2000

Members of the Kenneth A. Brett School Eighth Grade Class of 1999 - 2000. Seated from left are Sarah Wood, Kim White and Abby Creps. Standing are John Perkins, Media Specialist, Craig Anthony, Tyson Nourse, Mackenzie Maher-Coville, Adam Robinson, Mike Marrone, and Social Studies teacher, Brian P. Wiggin.

PREFACE BY THE STUDENTS

We, the eighth grade class of the Kenneth A. Brett School in Tamworth, NH, are reprinting this book in order for more New Hampshire citizens and all Americans to learn about the only president who was born in our state, Franklin Pierce. When our social studies teacher, Mr. Wiggin, tried to find the book in our school library he discovered that we did not have a copy of it. He then called the State Library to see if they had any copies. They did, but only one. He asked for a copy, and Councilor Ray Burton and State Librarian Michael York made a photocopy of the book which they sent to us. Mr. Wiggin then came up with the idea to have the book reprinted and we decided to use the money we have earned from the Boxtops for Education program to pay for it. Our Tamworth School Board endorsed the idea so that we could get started without raising all the money ahead of time.

Reprinting this book is a good idea for more than one reason. One, this book is incredibly rare. Two, the biography is rare enough that most people don't even know the book exists. Three, it is a book which tells a lot about Franklin Pierce and shows what good friends he and Nathaniel Hawthorne were. We think you can find out more about Pierce and the history of his times from reading this short 1852 book than from reading some of the more modern books about Pierce. After this project was endorsed by the school board, we downloaded the text of the book that had been loaded onto the internet. We then proofread the internet version using our photocopy of the original to make sure our version would be accurate.

After this part of the project was completed, we made field trips to Concord, and to Hillsborough to visit the Pierce Manse, the New Hampshire Historical Society, the North Main Street Cemetery, his burial site, and the Pierce Homestead. Here we collected material for the project to illustrate the book. When we were done, all of us knew more about Franklin Pierce than we knew about any other president.

   This was a valuable learning experience for all of us who worked on this book. Not only have we learned more about the life of Franklin Pierce, but we also learned the steps involved in getting a book published. We hope you appreciate our efforts.

Sincerely,
The Eighth Grade Class at the Kenneth A. Brett School
Tamworth, NH
May 2000.

Eighth Graders who worked on the Pierce Biography

Nicole Anderson, Craig Anthony, Jason Cameron, Sydra Cooperdock, Abby Creps, Trevor Curtin, Brittany Ellis, Jen Fawson, Kevin Foss, Jamie Griffin, Kelly Hamaleinen, Hilary Jaworski, Arnie Krupula, Mackenzie Maher-Coville, Mike Marrone, Joshua Mason, Tyson Nourse, Megan O'Kelly, Danny Paquette, Adam Robinson, Aaron Shaw, Erin Slattery, Norman Stelbergs, Matt Stewart, Kim White, Stacey White, Becky Wilcox, and Sarah Wood

Class of 2001 who worked on the Index
Sean Ashe, Jennie Bonica, Matt Hamel, Heidi Noriegg, Julie Streeter.

WHAT WE THINK ABOUT
FRANKLIN PIERCE

Franklin Pierce was a very sad man. He accomplished a lot in his lifetime while other people conspired to hurt him. He was a man who watched his three sons die and then outlived his wife. All of his decisions were based on ideas that he really believed in, but while he was alive nobody believed this and accused him of everything they could think of. Pierce should be respected more for what he tried to do even if he wasn't as successful as other Presidents were.

Abraham Lincoln is supposed to be the greatest president. You could say that Franklin Pierce did things more by what he believed than Lincoln did. Pierce believed that states should be able to decide if slavery was legal. So did Lincoln. Now historians say that Pierce was a failure because everything he did was pro-slavery. Slavery was the law at the time, and Pierce was upholding the law. Pierce believed in the law, not in hurting the slaves. Lincoln was not an abolitionist and probably would not have freed the slaves with the Emancipation Proclamation if he hadn't been forced to by the war. So you could make a case that Pierce acted because of ideas that he believed in when he signed the Kansas-Nebraska Act and say that Lincoln signed the Emancipation Proclamation because the country made him do it.

The majority of people in America agreed with Pierce about slavery for most of his lifetime. Radicals could have started the Civil War before Pierce was president. It could have started in 1850 without the compromise worked out in Congress. All of Pierce's decisions were based on what he believed. When he started, the majority of Americans agreed with him, but slowly more and more people decided that the other side was evil. Both sides thought they were right and became more and more radical. Lincoln wasn't a radical but he had to make the decisions that many of the radicals wanted him to make. Lincoln wanted to stop the war but wasn't able to. If this was impossible for Lincoln it was impossible for Pierce, too.

Pierce worked hard for his country as a soldier, a congressman, a senator, and as president. He was a man of courage and strong beliefs. New Hampshire gave the nation a very good man to be president. Anybody who thinks Franklin Pierce did a bad job should spend more time reading about him. While we were reading about Franklin Pierce in this biography, we were sad that later people blamed him for many things that he couldn't have changed. We learned to like Pierce the best of all the presidents because after visiting his homes and seeing things that belonged to him we know more about him than any of the other presidents. We hope reading this book will get you to respect Franklin Pierce.

Jason Cameron
Eighth Grade Class, 2000
K.A. Brett School

Franklin Pierce Chronology

1804   Franklin Pierce was born November 23. His place of birth was Hillsborough, N.H. Pierce's religious denomination was Episcopalian.

1818-20 Attended Hancock Academy, Hancock, N.H.

1820   Entered Bowdoin College, Brunswick, ME, October 4.

1824   Graduated from Bowdoin, October.

1825   Elected to Phi Beta Kappa Society, Bowdoin.

1829   Elected to N.H. Legislature. Appointed Justice of the Peace, Hillsborough, May.

1833   Elected to the U.S. House of Representatives.

1834   Married to Jane Means Appleton, November 19.

1836   First son, Franklin is born February second and dies on February fifth.

1837   Elected to U.S. Senate and becomes the youngest senator.

1839   Father Benjamin Pierce dies. Second son Frank Robert Pierce is born, August 27.

1841   Third son, Benjamin Pierce is born, April 13.

1843   Frank Robert Pierce dies, November 14.

1844   Appointed District Attorney for N.H. by James K. Polk.

1847   Joins General Scott at Puebla de Zaragoza as commissioned officer in the US Army.

1850   Elected President of State Constitutional Convention.

1852   Nominated for President by the Democratic Party, June 4.

Wins the election after highly contentious campaign, November.

1853   Son, Benjamin is killed in a train wreck near Andover, MA on January sixth, shortly before the inauguration.

Signs the Gadsden Purchase agreement acquiring land in the southwest

1854   Kansas-Nebraska Act allows the two territories self determination on the issue of slavery.

1856   Denied the nomination for the Presidency by the Democratic Party.

First Christmas tree is set up in the White House.

1857   Returns to Concord, N.H.

1858   Tours France, England, and Italy with Jane and meets Hawthorne in Rome.

1863   Nathaniel Hawthorne dedicates his last book, *Our Old Home* to Pierce.

Jane Means Appleton Pierce dies on December second.

1864   Pierce challenged by mob as a traitor at his home in Concord.

1865   Becomes demoralized and drinks heavily.

1869   Dies in Concord at age 64 of stomach inflammation.

NATHANIEL HAWTHORNE CHRONOLOGY

1804 Born in Salem, MA, July 4.

1821-5 Attends Bowdoin College.

Writes the following books:
1828 *Fanshawe*
1831 *Gentle Boy*
1832 *Roger Malvin's Burial*
1834 *Mr. Higginbotham's Catastrophe*
1837 *Twice-Told Tales*

1842 Marries Sophia Peabody and settles in Concord, MA.

Lives in a literary colony with Ralph Waldo Emerson and A. Bronson Alcott.

1846-9 Works in the U.S. Custom House at Salem, MA as Port Surveyor.

Writes:
1846 *Mosses from an Old Manse*
1850 *The Scarlet Letter*
      The Great Stone Face
1851 *The House of Seven Gables*
      Snow-Image and Other Twice-Told Tales
1852 *Blithedale Romance*

Writes *The Life of Franklin Pierce* at the request of the candidate.

1853   Appointed by Franklin Pierce as the US Consul at
          Liverpool, England.

1853-60 Lives at Liverpool and elsewhere abroad.

1864   Dies in Plymouth, N.H, with Franklin Pierce at his side.
          Buried in Sleepy Hollow Cemetery in Concord, MA.

The Pierce Manse is shown here from the front. Pierce spent many days of his life here.

Our class took many trips to Concord, N.H., to take pictures and learn more about Franklin Pierce's life. Shown here is a sign marking where the Pierce Manse is located and facts about his old home.

Here is our class visiting the Franklin Pierce Memorial in Concord, N.H. In front (starting at left) are students Craig Anthony, Aaron Shaw, Tyson Nourse, teacher Brian P. Wiggin, and Norman Stelberg.

This sign sits outside the North Main Street Cemetery in Concord where Pierce is buried and commemorates his life and accomplishments.

Here are members of the class responsible for illustrations. From left are Kim White, Craig Anthony, Mackenzie Maher-Coville, Doug Copely, curator at the Museum of New Hampshire History, and Brian P. Wiggin, teacher. We are seen admiring a plaster bust of Franklin Pierce. Behind the camera is Kenneth A. Brett School Librarian, John Perkins, who helped a great deal with the photography and the book.

Here is Douglas Copely, Curator, who assisted with the photographs taken at the museum. We were honored to be able to photograph these rare items in the collection, which are not on permanent display and are made available only to those doing serious research.

Seen here are two medals, bronze on left and silver on the right. Except for the metals used, the medals are identical, the bronze showing the face and the silver showing the obverse. These Indian Peace Medals, which were passed out to peaceful Indian tribes. The hole drilled in the top of the silver medal signifies that it was worn around the neck of a Native American chieftain.

Shown here are campaign materials, (top) a Pierce and King campaign knife, and a campaign poster. On the left is Pierce and on the right is William R. King.

Shown here are a maroon silk sash owned by Franklin Pierce and worn while he was in office, and a rosewood, gold-topped cane used by Pierce during his presidency.

(above) Shown here is a brooch (left) belonging to Mrs. Franklin Pierce, supposedly containing Mrs. Alexander Hamilton's hair, and a fan also belonging to Mrs. Pierce. The fan's handle and base is made of ivory and covered with violet silk. Embroidered on the silk in a floral pattern are small glass sequins. (below)Here are some artifacts owned by Franklin Pierce. From the left a gilt ceremonial sword presented to Pierce, another ceremonial sword, nickel with brass fittings, a hat worn by Pierce in the Mexican American War, and two pairs of epaulettes worn by Pierce as General in the U.S. Army.

Here is a plaster bust of Franklin Pierce shown in profile. Pierce was considered to be extremely handsome by his contemporaries and was nicknamed "Handsome Frank."

From left are a campaign medal and ribbon owned by Pierce and a gold and ivory pen used by Pierce to sign the Kansas-Nebraska Act. The pen is emblematic of the lofty hopes which Pierce had for the legislation which is now thought to be responsible for the time known as Bloody Kansas, a period of great suffering and grief for those on the frontier.

From top left are a miniature portrait of Franklin Pierce on ivory, a gold brooch belonging to Mrs. Franklin Pierce, and two gold watch fobs used by Franklin Pierce which represented his membership in the Society of Cincinnati. Watch fobs were men's jewelry, which were seen on a gentleman's vest suspended from a fancy watch chain.

Here is a hand colored engraving of Franklin Pierce, presumably holding a copy of the Missouri Compromise. This legislation was highly respected by Pierce's contemporaries who believed that it would assure peace for the next generation.

The Life
of
Franklin Pierce

by

Nathaniel Hawthorne

1852

Nathaniel Hawthorne by artist G.P.A. Healey.

PREFACE

THE AUTHOR of this memoir—being so little of a politician that he scarcely feels entitled to call himself a member of any party—would not voluntarily have undertaken the work here offered to the public. Neither can he flatter himself that he has been remarkably successful in the performance of his task, viewing it in the light of a political biography, and as a representation of the principles and acts of a public man, intended to operate upon the minds of multitudes, during a presidential canvass. This species of writing is too remote from his customary occupations —and, he may add, from his tastes—to be very satisfactorily done, without more time and practice than he would be willing to expend for such a purpose. If this little biography have any value, it is probably of another kind —as the narrative of one who knew the individual of whom he treats, at a period of life when character could be read with undoubting accuracy, and who, consequently, in judging of the motives of his subsequent conduct has an advantage over much more competent observers, whose knowledge of the man may have commenced at a later date. Nor can it be considered improper, (at least the author will never feel it so, although some foolish delicacy be sacrificed in the undertaking,) that when a friend, dear to him almost from boyish days, stands up before his country, misrepresented by indiscriminate abuse, on the one hand, and by aimless praise, on the other, be should be sketched by one who has had opportunities of knowing him well, and who is certainly inclined to tell the truth.

It is perhaps right to say, that while this biography is so far sanc-
tioned by General Pierce, as it comprises a generally correct narrative
of the principal events of his life, the author does not understand him
as thereby necessarily indorsing all the sentiments put forth by himself, in the progress of the work. These are the author's own specula-
tions upon the facts before him, and may, or may not, be in accordance with the ideas of the individual whose life he writes. That individual's opinions, however, —so far as it is necessary to know them,—
may be read, in his straightforward and consistent deeds, with more
certainty than those of almost any other man now before the public.

The author, while collecting his materials, has received liberal aid
from all manner of people—whigs and democrats, congressmen,
astute lawyers, grim old generals of militia, and gallant young officers
of the Mexican war—most of whom, however, he must needs say,
have rather abounded in eulogy, of General Pierce, than in such anec-
dotical matter as is calculated for a biography. Among the gentlemen
to whom be is substantially indebted, he would mention Hon. C. G.
Atherton, Hon. S. H. Ayer, Hon. Joseph Hall, Chief Justice Gilchrist,
Isaac 0. Barnes, Esq., Col. T. J. Whipple, and Mr. C. J. Smith. He has
likewise derived much assistance from an able and accurate sketch,
that originally appeared in the *Boston Post* and was drawn up, as he
believes, by the junior editor of that journal.

CONCORD, (Mass.,) August 27, 1852.

1

HIS PARENTAGE AND EARLY LIFE

FRANKLIN PIERCE was born at Hillsborough, in the State of New Hampshire, on the 23d of November, 1804. His native county, at the period of his birth, covered a much more extensive territory than at present, and might reckon among its children many memorable men, and some illustrious ones. General Stark, the hero of Bennington, Daniel Webster, Levi Woodbury, Jeremiah Smith, the eminent jurist, and governor of the state, General James Miller, General McNeil, Senator Atherton, were natives of old Hillsborough county.

General Benjamin Pierce, the father of Franklin, was one of the earliest settlers in the town of Hillsborough, and contributed as much as any other man to the growth and prosperity of the county. He was born in 1757, at Chelmsford, now Lowell, in Massachusetts. Losing his parents early, he grew up under the care of an uncle, amid such circumstances of simple fare, hard labor, and scanty education as usually fell to the lot of a New England yeoman's family some eighty or a hundred years ago. On the 19th of April, 1775, being then less than eighteen years of age, the stripling was at the plough, when tidings reached him of the bloodshed at Lexington and Concord. He immediately loosened the ox chain, left the plough in the furrow, took his uncle's gun and equipments, and set forth towards the scene of action. From that day, for more than seven years, he never saw his native place. He enlisted in the army, was present at the battle of Bunker Hill, and after serving through the whole revolutionary war, and fighting his way upward from the lowest grade, returned, at last, a thorough soldier, and commander of a company. He was retained in the army as long as that body of veterans had a united existence; and, being finally disbanded, at West Point, in 1784, was left with no other reward, for nine years of toil and danger, than the nominal amount of his pay in the Continental currency—then so depreciated as to be almost worthless.

In 1785, being employed as agent to explore a tract of wild land, he purchased a lot of fifty acres in what is now the town of Hillsborough. In the spring of the succeeding year, he built himself a log hut, and began the clearing and cultivation of his tract. Another year beheld him married to his first wife, Elizabeth Andrews, who died within a twelvemonth after their union, leaving a daughter, the present widow of General John McNeil. In 1789, he married Anna Kendrick, with whom he lived about half a century, and who bore him eight children, of whom Franklin was the sixth.

Although the revolutionary soldier had thus betaken himself to the wilderness for a subsistence, his professional merits were not forgotten by those who had witnessed his military career. As early as 1786, he was appointed brigade major of the militia of Hillsborough county, then first organized and formed into a brigade. And it was a still stronger testimonial to his character as a soldier, that, nearly fifteen years afterwards, during the presidency of John Adams, he was offered a high command in the northern division of the army which was proposed to be levied in anticipation of a war with the French republic. Inflexibly democratic in his political faith, however, Major Pierce refused to be implicated in a policy which he could not approve. "No, gentlemen," said he to the delegates, who urged his acceptance of the commission, "poor as I am, and acceptable as would be the position under other circumstances, I would sooner go to yonder mountains, dig me a cave, and live on roast potatoes, than be instrumental in promoting the objects for which that army is to be raised!" This same fidelity to his principles marked every public, as well as private, action of his life.

In his own neighborhood, among those who knew him best, he early gained an influence that was never lost nor diminished, but continued to spread wider during the whole of his long life. In 1789, he was elected to the state legislature, and retained that position for thirteen successive years, until chosen a member of the council. During the same period, he was active in his military duties, as a field officer, and finally general, of the militia of the county; and Miller, McNeil, and others, learned of him, in this capacity, the soldier-like discipline which was afterwards displayed on the battle fields of the northern frontier.

The history, character, and circumstances of General Benjamin Pierce, though here but briefly touched upon, are essential parts of the biography of his son, both as indicating some of the native traits which the latter has inherited, and as showing the influences amid which he grew up. At Franklin Pierce's birth, and for many years subsequent, his father was the most active and public-spirited man within his sphere; a most decided democrat, and supporter of Jefferson and Madison; a practical farmer, moreover, not rich, but independent, exercising a liberal hospitality, and noted for the kindness and generosity of his character; a man of the people, but whose natural qualities inevitably made him a leader among them. From infancy upward, the boy had before his eyes, as the model on which he might instinctively form himself, one of the best specimens of sterling New England character, developed in a life of simple habits, yet of elevated action. Patriotism, such as it had been in revolutionary days, was taught him by his father, as early as his mother taught him religion. He became early imbued, too, with the military spirit which the old soldier had retained from his long service, and which was kept active by the constant alarms and warlike preparations of the first twelve years of the present century. If any man is bound, by birth and youthful training, to show himself a brave, faithful, and able citizen of his native country, it is the son of such a father.

At the commencement of the war of 1812, Franklin Pierce was a few months under eight years of age. The old general, his father, sent two of his sons into the army; and, as his eldest daughter was soon afterwards married to Major McNeil, there were few families that had so large a personal stake in the war as that of General Benjamin Pierce. He himself, both in his public capacity as a member of the council, and by his great local influence in his own county, lent a strenuous support to the national administration. It is attributable to his sagacity and energy, that New Hampshire—then under a federal governor—was saved the disgrace of participation in the questionable, if not treasonable, projects of the Hartford Convention. He identified himself with the cause of the country, and was doubtless as thoroughly alive with patriotic zeal, at this eventful period, as in the old days of Bunker Hill, and Saratoga, and Yorktown. The general not only took a prominent part at all public meetings, but was ever ready for the informal discussion of political affairs at all places of casual resort, where—in accordance with the custom of the time and country—the minds of men were made to operate effectually upon each other. Franklin Pierce was a frequent auditor of these controversies. The intentness with which he watched the old general, and listened to his arguments, is still remembered; and, at this day, in his most earnest moods, there are gesticulations and movements that bring up the image of his father to those who recollect the latter on those occasions of the display of homely, native eloquence. No mode of education could be conceived, better adapted to imbue a youth with the principles and sentiment of democratic institutions; it brought him into the most familiar contact with the popular mind, and made his own mind a part of it.

Franklin's father had felt, through life, the disadvantages of a defective education; although, in his peculiar sphere of action, it might be doubted whether he did not gain more than he lost, by being thrown on his own resources, and compelled to study men and their actual affairs, rather than books. But he determined to afford his son all the opportunities of improvement, which he himself had lacked. Franklin, accordingly, was early sent to the academy at Hancock, and afterwards to that of Francestown, where he was received into the family of General Pierce's old and steadfast friend, Peter Woodbury, father of the late eminent judge. It is scarcely more than a year ago, at the semi-centennial celebration of the academy, that Franklin Pierce, the mature and distinguished man, paid a beautiful tribute to the character of Madam Woodbury, in affectionate remembrance of the motherly kindness experienced at her hands by the schoolboy.

The old people of his neighborhood give a very delightful picture of Franklin at this early age. They describe him as a beautiful boy, with blue eyes, light curling hair, and a sweet expression of face. The traits presented of him indicate moral symmetry, kindliness, and a delicate texture of sentiment, rather than marked prominences of character. His instructors testify to his propriety of conduct, his fellow-pupils to his sweetness of disposition and cordial sympathy. One of the latter, being older than most of his companions, and less advanced in his studies, found it difficult to keep up with his class; and he remembers how perseveringly, while the other boys were at play, Franklin spent the noon recess, for many weeks together, in aiding him in his lessons. These attributes, proper to a generous and affectionate nature, have remained with him through life. Lending their color to his deportment, and softening his manners, they are, perhaps, even now, the characteristics by which most of those who casually meet him would be inclined to identify the man. But there are other qualities, not then developed, but which have subsequently attained a firm and manly growth, and are recognized as his leading traits among those who really know him. Franklin Pierce's development, indeed, has always been the reverse of premature; the boy did not show the germ of all that was in the man, nor, perhaps, did the young man adequately foreshow the mature one.

In 1820, at the age of sixteen, he became a student of Bowdoin College, at Brunswick, Maine. It was in the autumn of the next year, that the author of this memoir entered the class below him; but our college reminiscences, however interesting to the parties concerned, are not exactly the material for a biography. He was then a youth, with the boy and man in him, vivacious, mirthful, slender, of a fair complexion, with light hair that had a curl in it: his bright and cheerful aspect made a kind of sunshine, both as regarded its radiance and its warmth; insomuch that no shyness of disposition, in his associates, could well resist its influence. We soon became acquainted, and were more especially drawn together as members of the same college society. There were two of these institutions, dividing the college between them, and typifying, respectively, and with singular accuracy of feature, the respectable conservative, and the progressive or democratic parties. Pierce's native tendencies inevitably drew him to the latter.

His chum was Zenas Caldwell, several years elder than himself, a member of the Methodist persuasion, a pure-minded, studious, devoutly religious character; endowed thus early in life with the authority of a grave and sagacious turn of mind. The friendship between Pierce and him appeared to be mutually strong, and was of itself a pledge of correct deportment in the former. His chief friend, I think, was a classmate named Little, a young man of most estimable qualities, and high intellectual promise; one of those fortunate characters whom an early death so canonizes in the remembrance of their companions, that the perfect fulfillment of a long life would scarcely give them a higher place. Jonathan Cilley, of my own class,—whose untimely fate is still mournfully remembered,—a person of very marked ability and great social influence, was another of Pierce's friends. All these have long been dead. There are others, still alive, who would meet Franklin Pierce, at this day, with as warm a pressure of the hand, and the same confidence in his kindly feelings, as when they parted from him, nearly thirty years ago.

Pierce's class was small, but composed of individuals seriously intent on the duties and studies of their college life. They were not boys, but for the most part, well advanced towards maturity; and, having wrought out their own means of education, were little inclined to neglect the opportunities that had been won at so much cost. They knew the value of time, and had a sense of the responsibilities of their position. Their first scholar—the present Professor Stowe—has long since established his rank among the first scholars of the country. It could have been no easy task to hold successful rivalry with students so much in earnest as these were. During the earlier part of his college course, it may be doubted whether Pierce was distinguished for scholarship. But, for the last two years, be appeared to grow more intent on the business in hand, and, without losing any of his vivacious qualities as a companion, was evidently resolved to gain an honorable elevation in his class. His habits of attention, and obedience to college discipline, were of the strictest character; he rose progressively in scholarship, and took a highly creditable degree.

The first civil office, I imagine, which Franklin Pierce ever held, was that of chairman of the standing committee of the Athenaean Society, of which, as above hinted, we were both members; and, having myself held a place on the committee, I can bear testimony to his having discharged not only his own share of the duties, but, that of his colleagues. I remember, likewise, that the only military service of my life was as a private soldier in a college company, of which Pierce was one of the officers. He entered into this latter business, or pastime, with an earnestness with which I could not pretend to compete, and at which, perhaps, he would now be inclined to smile. His slender and youthful figure rises before my mind's eye, at this moment, with the air and step of a veteran of the school of Steuben ; as well became the son of a revolutionary hero, who had probably drilled under the old baron's orders. Indeed, at this time, and for some years afterwards, Pierce's ambition seemed to be of a military cast. Until reflection had tempered his first predilections, and other varieties of success had rewarded his efforts, he would have preferred, I believe, the honors of the battle field to any laurels more peacefully won. And it was remarkable how, with all the invariable gentleness of his demeanor, he perfectly gave, nevertheless, the impression of a high and fearless spirit. His friends were as sure of his courage, while yet untried, as now, when it has been displayed so brilliantly in famous battles.

At this early period of his life, he was distinguished by the same fascination of manner that has since proved so magical in winning him an unbounded personal popularity. It is wronging him, however, to call this peculiarity a mere effect of manner; its source lies deep in the kindliness of his nature, and in the liberal, generous, catholic sympathy, that embraces all who are worthy of it. Few men possess any thing like it; so irresistible as it is, so sure to draw forth an undoubting confidence, and so true to the promise which it gives. This frankness, this democracy of good feeling, has not been chilled by the society of politicians, nor polished down into mere courtesy, by his intercourse with the most refined men of the day. It belongs to him at this moment, and will never leave him. A little while ago, after his return from Mexico, he darted across the street to exchange a hearty gripe of the hand with a rough countryman upon his cart—a man who used to "live with his father," as the general explained the matter to his companions. Other men assume this manner, more or less skillfully; but with Frank Pierce it is an innate characteristic; nor will it ever lose its charm unless his heart should grow narrower and colder—a misfortune not to be anticipated, even in the dangerous atmosphere of elevated rank, whither he seems destined to ascend.

There is little else that it is worth while to relate, as regards his college course, unless it be, that, during one of his winter vacations, Pierce taught a country school. So many of the statesmen of New England have performed their first public service in the character of pedagogue, that it seems almost a necessary step on the ladder of advancement.

2

HIS SERVICES IN THE STATE AND NATIONAL LEGISLATURES

AFTER leaving college, in the year 1824, Franklin Pierce returned to Hillsborough. His father, now in a green old age, continued to take a prominent part in the affairs of the day, but likewise made his declining years rich and picturesque with recollections of the heroic times through which he had lived. On the 26th of December, 1825, it being his sixty-seventh birthday, General Benjamin Pierce prepared a festival for his comrades in arms, the survivors of the revolution, eighteen of whom, all inhabitants of Hillsborough, assembled at his house. The ages of these veterans ranged from fifty-nine up to the patriarchal venerableness of nearly ninety. They spent the day in festivity, in calling up reminiscences of the great men whom they had known, and the great deeds which they had helped to do, and in reviving the old sentiments of the era of seventy-six. At nightfall, after a manly and pathetic farewell from their host, they separated— "prepared," as the old general expressed it, "at the first tap of the shrouded drum, to move and join their beloved Washington, and the rest of their comrades, who fought and bled at their sides." A scene like this must have been profitable for a young man to witness, as being likely to give him a stronger sense, than most of us can attain, of the value of that Union which these old heroes had risked so much to consolidate—of that common country which they had sacrificed every thing to create; and patriotism must have been communicated from their hearts to his with somewhat of the warmth and freshness of a new-born sentiment. No youth was ever more fortunate than Franklin Pierce, through the whole of his early life, in this most desirable species of moral education.

Having chosen the law as a profession, Franklin became a student in the office of Judge Woodbury, of Portsmouth. Allusion has already been made to the friendship between General Benjamin Pierce and Peter Woodbury, the father of the judge. The early progress of Levi Woodbury towards eminence had been facilitated by the powerful influence of his father's friend. It was a worthy and honorable kind of patronage, and bestowed only as the great abilities of the recipient vindicated his claim to it. Few young men have met with such early success in life, or have deserved it so eminently, as did Judge Woodbury. At the age of twenty-seven, he was appointed to the bench of the Supreme Court of the state, on the earnest recommendation of old General Pierce. The opponents of the measure ridiculed him as the "baby judge;" but his conduct in that high office showed the pre-scient judgment of the friend who had known him from a child, and had seen in his young manhood already the wisdom of ripened age. It was some years afterwards when Franklin Pierce entered the office of Judge Woodbury as a student. In the interval, the judge had been elected governor, and, after a term of office that thoroughly tested the integrity of his democratic principles, had lost his second election, and returned to the profession of the law.

The last two years of Pierce's preparatory studies were spent at the law school of Northampton, in Massachusetts, and in the office of Judge Parker at Amherst. In 1827, being admitted to the bar, he began the practice of his profession at Hillsborough. It is an interesting fact, considered in reference to his subsequent splendid career as an advocate, that he did not, at the outset, give promise of distinguished success. His first case was a failure, and perhaps a somewhat marked one. But it is remembered that this defeat, however mortifying at the moment, did but serve to make him aware of the latent resources of his mind, the full command of which he was far from having yet attained. To a friend, an older practitioner, who addressed him with some expression of condolence and encouragement, Pierce replied,—

and it was a kind of self-assertion which no triumph would have drawn out, "I do not need that. I will try nine hundred and ninety-nine cases, if clients will continue to trust me, and, if I fail just as I have to-day, will try the thousandth. I shall live to argue cases in this court house in a manner that will mortify neither myself nor my friends." It is in such moments of defeat that character and ability are most fairly tested; they would irremediably crush a youth devoid of real energy, and being neither more nor less than his just desert, would be accepted as such. But a failure of this kind serves an opposite purpose to a mind in which the strongest and richest qualities lie deep, and, from their very size and mass, cannot at once be rendered available. It provokes an innate self-confidence, while, at the same time, it sternly indicates the sedulous cultivation, the earnest effort, the toil, the agony, which are the conditions of ultimate success. It is, indeed, one of the best modes of discipline that experience can administer, and may reasonably be counted a fortunate event in the life of a young man vigorous enough to overcome the momentary depression.

Pierce's distinction at the bar, however, did not immediately follow; nor did he acquire what we may designate as positive eminence until some years after this period. The enticements of political life—so especially fascinating to a young lawyer, but so irregular in its tendencies and so inimical to steady professional labor—had begun to operate upon him. His father's prominent position in the politics of the state made it almost impossible that the son should stand aloof. In 1827, the same year when Franklin began the practice of the law, General Benjamin Pierce had been elected governor of New Hampshire. He was defeated in the election of 1828, but was again successful in that of the subsequent year. During these years, the contest for the presidency had been fought with a fervor that drew almost every body into it, on one side or the other, and had terminated in the triumph of Andrew Jackson. Franklin Pierce, in advance of his father's decision, though not in opposition to it, had declared himself for the illustrious man, whose military renown was destined to be thrown into the shade by a civil administration the most splendid and powerful that ever adorned the annals of our country. I love to record of the subject of this memoir, that his first political faith was pledged to that great leader of the democracy.

I remember meeting Pierce, about this period, and catching from him some faint reflection of the zeal with which he was now stepping into the political arena. My sympathies and opinions, it is true,—so far as I had any in public affairs,—had, from the first, been enlisted on the same side with his own. But I was now made strongly sensible of an increased development of my friend's mind, by means of which he possessed a vastly greater power, than heretofore, over the minds with which he came in contact. This progressive growth has continued to be one of his remarkable characteristics. Of most men you early know the mental gauge and measurement, and do not subsequently have much occasion to change it. Not so with Pierce: his tendency was not merely high, but towards a point which rose higher and higher, as the aspirant tended upward. Since we parted, studious days had educated him; life, too, and his own exertions in it, and his native habit of close and accurate observation, had likewise begun to educate him.

The town of Hillsborough, in 1829, gave Franklin Pierce his first public honor, by electing him its representative in the legislature of the state. His whole service in that body comprised four years, in the two latter of which he was elected speaker by a vote of one hundred and fifty-five, against fifty-eight for other candidates. This over-powering majority evinced the confidence which his character inspired, and which, during his whole career, it has invariably commanded, in advance of what might be termed positive proof, although the result has never failed to justify it. I still recollect his description of the feelings with which he entered on his arduous duties—the feverish night that preceded his taking the chair—the doubt, the struggle with himself—all ending in perfect calmness, full self-possession, and free power of action, when the crisis actually came.

He had all the natural gifts that adapted him for the post; courtesy, firmness, quickness and accuracy of judgment, and a clearness of mental perception that brought its own regularity into the scene of confused and entangled debate; and to these qualities he added whatever was to be attained by laborious study of parliamentary rules. His merit as a presiding officer was universally acknowledged. It is rare that a man combines so much impulse with so great a power of regulating the impulses of himself and others as Franklin Pierce. The faculty, here exercised and improved, of controlling an assembly while agitated by tumultuous controversy, was afterwards called into play upon a higher field; for, during his congressional service, Pierce was often summoned to preside in committee of the whole, when a turbulent debate was expected to demand peculiar energy in the chair.

He was elected a member of Congress in 1833; being young for the station, as he has always been for every public station that he has filled. A different kind of man—a man conscious that accident alone had elevated him, and therefore nervously anxious to prove himself equal to his fortunes -would thus have been impelled to spasmodic efforts. He would have thrust himself forward in debate, taking the word out of the mouths of renowned orators, and thereby winning notoriety, as at least the glittering counterfeit of true celebrity. Had Pierce, with his genuine ability, practised this course, had he possessed even an ordinary love of display, and had he acted upon it with his inherent tact and skill, taking advantage of fair occasions to prove the power and substance that were in him, it would greatly have facilitated the task of his biographer.

To aim at personal distinction, however, as an object independent of the public service, would have been contrary to all the foregone and subsequent manifestations of his life. He was never wanting to the occasion; but he waited for the occasion to bring him inevitably forward. When he spoke, it was not only because he was fully master of the subject, but because the exigency demanded him, and because no other and older man could perform the same duty as well as himself. Of the copious eloquence—and some of it, no doubt, of a high order—which Buncombe has called forth, not a paragraph, nor a period, is attributable to Franklin Pierce. He had no need of these devices to fortify his constituents in their high opinion of him; nor did he fail to perceive that such was not the method to acquire real weight in the body of which he was a member. In truth, he has no fluency of words, except when an earnest meaning and purpose supply their own expression. Every one of his speeches in Congress, and, we may say, in every other hall of oratory, or on any stump that he may have mounted, was drawn forth by the perception that it was needed, was directed to a full exposition of the subject, and (rarest of all) was limited by what he really had to say. Even the graces of the orator were never elaborated, never assumed for their own sake, but were legitimately derived from the force of his conceptions, and from the impulsive warmth which accompanies the glow of thought. Owing to these peculiarities,—for such, unfortunately, they may be termed, in reference to what are usually the characteristics of a legislative career,—his position before the country was less conspicuous than that of many men, who could claim nothing like Pierce's actual influence in the national councils. His speeches, in their muscular texture and close grasp of their subject, resembled the brief but pregnant arguments and expositions of the sages of the Continental Congress, rather than the immeasurable harangues which are now the order of the day.

His congressional life, though it made comparatively so little show, was full of labor, directed to substantial objects. He was a member of the judiciary and other important committees; and the drudgery of the committee room, where so much of the real public business of the country is transacted, fell in large measure to his lot. Thus, even as a legislator, he may be said to have been a man of deeds, not words; and when he spoke upon any subject with which his duty, as chairman or member of a committee, had brought him in relation, his words had the weight of deeds, from the meaning, the directness, and the truth, that he conveyed into them. His merits made themselves known and felt in the sphere where they were exercised; and he was early appreciated by one who seldom erred in his estimate of men, whether in their moral or intellectual aspect. His intercourse with President Jackson was frequent and free, and marked by friendly regard on the part of the latter. In the stormiest periods of his administration, Pierce came frankly to his aid. The confidence then established was never lost; and when Jackson was on his death bed, being visited by a gentleman from the north, (himself formerly a democratic member of Congress,) the old hero spoke with energy of Franklin Pierce's ability and patriotism, and remarked, as if with prophetic foresight of his young friend's destiny, that "the interests of the country would be safe in such hands."

One of President Jackson's measures, which had Pierce's approval and support, was his veto of the Maysville Road bill. This bill was part of a system of vast public works, principally railroads and canals, which it was proposed to undertake at the expense of the national treasury—a policy not then of recent origin, but which had been fostered by John Quincy Adams, and had attained a gigantic growth at the close of his presidency. The estimate of works undertaken, or projected, at the commencement of Jackson's administration, amounted to considerably more than a hundred millions of dollars. The expenditure of this enormous sum, and doubtless of other incalculable amounts, in progressive increase, was to be for purposes often of unascertained utility, and was to pass through the agents and officers of the federal government—a means of political corruption not safely to be trusted even in the purest hands. The peril to the individuality of the states, from a system tending so directly to consolidate the powers of government towards a common centre, was obvious. The result might have been, with the lapse of time and the increased activity of the disease, to place the capital of our federative Union in a position resembling that of imperial Rome, where each once independent state was a subject province, and all the highways of the world were said to meet in her forum. It was against this system, so dangerous to liberty, and to public and private integrity, that Jackson declared war, by the famous Maysville veto.

It would be an absurd interpretation of Pierce's course, in regard to this and similar measures, to suppose him hostile either to internal or coastwise improvements, so far as they may legitimately be the business of the general government. He was aware of the immense importance of our internal commerce, and was ever ready to vote such appropriations as might be necessary for promoting it, when asked for in an honest spirit, and at points where they were really needed. He doubted, indeed, the constitutional power of Congress to undertake, by building roads through the wilderness or opening unfrequented rivers, to create commerce where it did not yet exist ; but he never denied or questioned the right and duty to remove obstructions in the way of inland trade, and to afford it every facility, when the nature and necessity of things had brought it into genuine existence. And he agreed with the best and wisest statesmen in believing that this distinction involved the true principle on which legislation, for the purpose here discussed, should proceed.

While a member of the House of Representatives, he delivered a forcible speech against the bill authorizing appropriations for the Military Academy at West Point. He was decidedly opposed to that institution, as then and at present organized. We allude to the subject in illustration of the generous frankness with which, years afterwards, when the battle smoke of Mexico had baptized him also a soldier, he acknowledged himself in the wrong, and bore testimony to the brilliant services which the graduates of the Academy, trained to soldiership from boyhood, had rendered to their country. And if he has made no other such acknowledgment of past error, committed in his legislative capacity, it is but fair to believe that it is because his reason and conscience accuse him of no other wrong.

It was while in the lower house of Congress, that Franklin Pierce took that stand on the slavery question, from which he has never since swerved a hair's breadth. He fully recognized, by his votes and by his voice, the rights pledged to the south by the constitution. This, at the period when he so declared himself, was comparatively an easy thing to do. But when it became more difficult, when the first imperceptible movement of agitation had grown to be almost a convulsion, his course was still the same. Nor did he ever shun the obloquy that sometimes threatened to pursue the northern man, who dared to love that great and sacred reality—his whole, united, native country—better than the mistiness of a philanthropic theory.

He continued in the House of Representatives four years. If, at this period of his life, he rendered unobtrusive, though not unimportant, services to the public, it must also have been a time of vast intellectual advantage to himself. Amidst great national affairs, be was acquiring the best of all educations for future eminence and leadership. In the midst of statesmen, he grew to be a statesman. Studious, as all his speeches prove him to be, of history, he beheld it demonstrating itself before his eyes. As regards this sort of training, much of its good or ill effect depends on the natural force and depth of the man. Many, no doubt, by early mixture with politics, become the mere politicians of the moment,—a class of men sufficiently abundant among us,—acquiring only knack and cunning, which guide them tolerably well through immediate difficulties, without instructing them in the great rules of higher policy. But when the actual observation of public measures goes hand in hand with study, when the mind is capable of comparing the present with its analogies in the past, and of grasping the principle that belongs to both, this is to have history for a living tutor. If the student be fit for such instruction, he will be seen to act afterwards with the elevation of a high ideal, and with the expediency, the sagacity, the instinct of what is fit and practicable, which make the advantage of the man of actual affairs over the mere theorist.

And it was another advantage of his being brought early into the sphere of national interests, and continuing there for a series of years, that enabled him to overcome any narrow and sectional prejudices. Without loving New England less, he loved the broad area of the country more. He thus retained that equal sentiment of patriotism for the whole land, with which his father had imbued him, and which is perhaps apt to be impaired in the hearts of those who come late to the national legislature, after long training in the narrower fields of the separate states. His sense of the value of the Union, which had been taught him at the fireside, from earliest infancy, by the stories of patriotic valor that he there heard, was now strengthened by friendly association with its representatives from every quarter. It is this youthful sentiment of Americanism, so happily developed by after circumstances, that we see operating through all his public life, and making him as tender of what he considers due to the south, as of the rights of his own land of hills.

Franklin Pierce had scarcely reached the legal age for such elevation, when, in 1837, he was elected to the Senate of the United States.

He took his seat at the commencement of the presidency of Mr. Van Buren. Never before nor since has the Senate been more venerable for the array of veteran and celebrated statesmen, than at that time. Calhoun, Webster, and Clay, had lost nothing of their intellectual might. Benton, Silas Wright, Woodbury, Buchanan, and Walker, were members; and many even of the less eminent names were such as have gained historic place—men of powerful eloquence, and worthy to be leaders of the respective parties which they espoused. To this dignified body (composed of individuals some of whom were older in political experience than he in his mortal life) Pierce came as the youngest member of the Senate. With his usual tact, and exquisite sense of propriety, he saw that it was not the time for him to step forward prominently on this highest theatre in the land. He beheld these great combatants doing battle before the eyes of the nation, and engrossing its whole regards. There was hardly an avenue to reputation save what was occupied by one or another of those gigantic figures.

Modes of public service remained, however, requiring high ability, but with which few men of competent endowments would have been content to occupy themselves. Pierce had already demonstrated the possibility of obtaining an enviable position among his associates, without the windy notoriety which a member of Congress may readily manufacture for himself by the lavish expenditure of breath that had been better spared. In the more elevated field of the Senate, he pursued the same course as while a representative, and with more than equal results.

Among other committees, he was a member of that upon revolutionary pensions. Of this subject he made himself thoroughly master, and was recognized by the Senate as an unquestionable authority. In 1840, in reference to several bills for the relief of claimants under the pension law, he delivered a speech which finely illustrates as well the sympathies as the justice of the man, showing how vividly he could feel, and, at the same time, how powerless were his feelings to turn him aside from the strict line of public integrity. The merits and sacrifices of the people of the revolution have never been stated with more earnest gratitude than in the following passage:—

"I am not insensible, Mr. President, of the advantages with which claims of this character always come before Congress. They are supposed to be based on services for which no man entertains a higher estimate than myself—services beyond all praise, and above all price. But, while warm and glowing with the glorious recollections which a recurrence to that period of our history can never fail to awaken; while we cherish with emotions of pride, reverence, and affection the memory of those brave men who are no longer with us; while we provide, with a liberal hand, for such as survive, and for the widows of the deceased; while we would accord to the heirs, whether in the second or third generation, every dollar to which they can establish a just claim,—I trust we shall not in the strong current of our sympathies, forget what becomes us as the descendants of such men. They would teach us to legislate upon our judgment, upon our sober sense of right, and not upon our impulses or our sympathies. No, sir; we may act in this way, if we choose, when dispensing our own means, but we are not at liberty to do it when dispensing the means of our constituents.

"If we were to legislate upon our sympathies—yet more I will admit—if we were to yield to that sense of just and grateful remuneration which presses itself upon every man's heart, there would be scarcely a limit for our bounty. The whole exchequer could not answer the demand. To the patriotism, the courage, and the sacrifices of the people of that day, we owe, under Providence, all that we now most highly prize, and what we shall transmit to our children as the richest legacy they can inherit. The war of the revolution, it has been justly remarked, was not a war of armies merely—it was the war of nearly a whole people and such a people as the world had never before seen, in a death struggle for liberty.

"The losses, sacrifices, and sufferings of that period were common to all classes and condition of life. Those who remained at home suffered hardly less than those who entered upon the active strife. The aged father and mother underwent not less than the son, who would have been the comfort and stay of their declining years, now called to perform a yet higher duty—to follow the standard of his bleeding country. The young mother, with her helpless children, excites not less deeply our sympathies, contending with want, and dragging out years of weary and toilsome days and anxious nights, than the husband in the field following the fortunes of our arms without the common habiliments to protect his person, or the requisite sustenance to support his strength. Sir, I never think of that patient, enduring, self-sacrificing army, which crossed the Delaware in December, 1777, marching barefooted upon frozen ground to encounter the foe, and leaving bloody footprints for miles behind them—I never think of their sufferings during that terrible winter without involuntarily inquiring, Where then were the families? Who lit up the cheerful fire upon their hearths at home? Who spoke the word of comfort and encouragement? Nay, sir, who furnished protection from the rigors of winter, and brought them the necessary means of subsistence?

"The true and simple answer to these questions would disclose an amount of suffering and anguish, mental and physical, such as might not have been found in the ranks of the armies—not even in the severest trial of that fortitude which never faltered, and that power of endurance which seemed to know no limit. All this no man feel more deeply than I do. But they were common sacrifices in a common cause, ultimately crowned with the reward of liberty. They have an everlasting claim upon our gratitude, and are destined, as I trust, by their heroic example, to exert an abiding influence upon our latest posterity."

With this heartfelt recognition of the debt of gratitude due to those excellent men, the senator enters into an analysis of the claims presented and proves them to be void of justice. The whole speech is a good exponent of his character; full of the truest sympathy, but, above all things, just, and not to be misled, on the public behalf, by those impulses that would be most apt to sway the private man. The mere pecuniary amount, saved to the nation by his scrutiny into affairs of this kind, though great, was, after all, but a minor consideration. The danger lay in establishing a corrupt system, and placing a wrong precedent upon the statute book. Instances might be adduced, on the other hand, which show him not less scrupulous of the just rights of the claimants, than careful of the public interests.

Another subject upon which he came forward was the military establishment, and the natural defences of the country. In looking through the columns of the Congressional Globe, we find abundant evidences of Senator Pierce's laborious and unostentatious discharge of his duties—reports of committees, brief remarks, and, here and there, a longer speech, always full of matter, and evincing a thoroughly-digested knowledge of the subject. Not having been written out by himself, however, these speeches are no fair specimens of his oratory, except as regards the train of argument and substantial thought; and adhering very closely to the business in hand, they seldom present passages that could be quoted, without tearing them forcibly, as it were, out of the context, and thus mangling the fragments which we might offer to the reader. As we have already remarked, he seems, as a debater, to revive the old type of the Revolutionary Congress, or to bring back the noble days of the Long Parliament of England, before eloquence had become what it is now, a knack, and a thing valued for itself. Like those strenuous orators, he speaks with the earnestness of honest conviction, and out of the fervor of his heart, and because the occasion and his deep sense of it constrain him.

By the defeat of Mr. Van Buren, in the presidential election of 1840, the administration of government was transferred, for the first time in twelve years, to the whigs. An extra session of Congress was summoned to assemble in June, 1841, by President Harrison, who, however, died before it came together. At this extra session, it was the purpose of the whig party, under the leadership of Henry Clay, to overthrow all the great measures which the successive democratic administrations had established. The sub-treasury was to be demolished; a national bank was to be incorporated;. a high tariff of duties was to be imposed, for purposes of protection and abundant revenue. The whig administration possessed a majority, both in the Senate and the House. It was a dark period for the democracy, so long unaccustomed to defeat, and now beholding all that they had won for the cause of national progress, after the arduous struggle of so many years, apparently about to be swept away.

The sterling influence which Franklin Pierce now exercised is well described in the following remarks of the Hon. A.O. P. Nicholson:—

"The power of an organized minority was never more clearly exhibited than in this contest. The democratic senators acted in strict concert, meeting night after night for consultation, arranging their plan of battle, selecting their champions for the coming day, assigning to each man his proper duty, and looking carefully to the popular judgment for a final victory. In these consultations, no man's voice was heard with more profound respect than that of Franklin Pierce. His counsels were characterized by so thorough a knowledge of human nature, by so much solid common sense, by such devotion to democratic principles, that, although among the youngest of the senators, it was deemed important that all their conclusions should be submitted to his sanction.

"Although known to be ardent in his temperament, he was also known to act with prudence and caution. His impetuosity in debate was only the result of the deep convictions which controlled his mind. He enjoyed the unbounded confidence of Calhoun, Buchanan, Wright, Woodbury, Walker, King, Benton, and indeed of the entire democratic portion of the Senate. When he rose in the Senate or in the committee room, he was heard with the profoundest attention; and again and again was he greeted by these veteran democrats as one of our ablest champions. His speeches, during this session, will compare with those of any other senator. If it be asked, why he did not receive higher distinction, I answer, that such men as Calhoun, Wright, Buchanan, and Woodbury, were the acknowledged leaders of the democracy. The eyes of the nation were on them. The hopes of their party were reposed in them. The brightness of these luminaries was too great to allow the brilliancy of so young a man to attract especial attention. But ask any one of these veterans how Franklin Pierce ranked in the Senate, and he will tell you, that, to stand in the front rank for talents, eloquence, and statesmanship, he only lacked a few more years."

In the course of this session, he made a very powerful speech in favor of Mr. Buchanan's resolution, calling on the president to furnish the names of persons removed from office since the 4th of March, 1841. The whigs, in 1840, as in the subsequent canvass of 1848, had professed a purpose to abolish the system of official removals on account of political opinion, but, immediately on coming into power, had commenced a proscription infinitely beyond the example of the democratic party. This course, with an army of office seekers besieging the departments, was unquestionably difficult to avoid, and perhaps, on the whole, not desirable to be avoided. But it was rendered astounding by the sturdy effrontery with which the gentlemen in power denied that their present practice had falsified any of their past professions. A few of the closing paragraphs of Senator Pierce's highly effective speech, being more easily separable than the rest, may here be cited.

"One word more, and I leave this subject—a painful one to me, from the beginning to the end. The senator from North Carolina, in the course of his remarks, the other day, asked, 'Do gentlemen expect that their friends are to be retained in office against the will of the nation? Are they so unreasonable as to expect what the circumstances and the necessity of the case forbid?' What our expectations were is not the question now; but what were your pledges and promises before the people. On a previous occasion, the distinguished senator from Kentucky made a similar remark: 'An ungracious task, but the nation demands it! ' Sir, this demand of the nation,—this plea Of STATE NECESSITY,—let me tell gentlemen, is as old as the history of wrong and oppression. It has been the standing plea, the never-failing resort of despotism.

"The great Julius found it a convenient plea when he restored the dignity of the Roman Senate, but destroyed its independence. It gave countenance to, and justified, all the atrocities of the Inquisition in Spain. It forced out the stifled groans that issued from the Black Hole of Calcutta. It was written in tears upon the Bridge of Sighs in Venice, and pointed to those dark recesses upon whose gloomy thresholds there was never seen a returning footprint.

"It was the plea of the austere and ambitious Strafford, in the days of Charles I. It filled the Bastile of France, and lent its sanction to the terrible atrocities perpetrated there. It was this plea that snatched the mild, eloquent, and patriotic Camille Desmoulins from his young and beautiful wife, and hurried him to the guillotine, with thousands of others, equally unoffending and innocent. It was upon this plea that the greatest of generals, if not men,—you cannot mistake me,—I mean him, the presence of whose very ashes, within the last few months, sufficed to stir the hearts of a continent,—it was upon this plea that he abjured the noble wife who had thrown light and gladness around his humbler days, and, by her own lofty energies and high intellect, had encouraged his aspirations. It was upon this plea that he committed that worst and most fatal act of his eventful life. Upon this, too, he drew around his person the imperial purple. It has in all times, and every age, been the foe of liberty, and the indispensable stay of usurpation.

"Where were the chains of despotism ever thrown around the freedom of speech and of press, but on this plea of STATE NECESSITY? Let the spirit of Charles X. and of his ministers answer.

"It is cold, selfish, heartless, and has always been regardless of age, sex, condition, services, or any of the incidents of
life that appeal to patriotism or humanity. Wherever its
authority has been acknowledged, it has assailed men who
stood by their country when she needed strong arms and
bold hearts, and has assailed them when, maimed and disabled in her service, they could no longer brandish a weapon
in her defence. It has afflicted the feeble and dependent wife
for the imaginary faults of the husband. It has stricken down
Innocence in its beauty, Youth in its freshness, Manhood in its
vigor, and Age in its feebleness and decrepitude. Whatever
other plea or apology may be set up for the sweeping, ruthless
exercise of this civil guillotine at the present day, in the name
of LIBERTY let us be spared this fearful one of STATE
NECESSITY, in this early age of the republic, upon the floor
of the American Senate, in the face of a people yet free!"

In June, 1842, he signified his purpose of retiring from the Senate. It
was now more than sixteen years since the author of this sketch had
been accustomed to meet Frank Pierce (that familiar name, which the
nation is adopting as one of its household words) in habits of daily
intercourse. Our modes of life had since been as different as could well
be imagined; our culture and labor were entirely unlike; there was
hardly a single object or aspiration in common between us. Still we
had occasionally met, and always on the old ground of friendly confidence. There were sympathies that had not been suffered to die out.
Had we lived more constantly together, it is not impossible that the
relation might have been changed by the various accidents and attri-
tions of life; but having no mutual events, and few mutual interests, the
tie of early friendship remained the same as when we parted. The
modifications which I saw in his character were those of growth and
development; new qualities came out, or displayed themselves more
prominently, but always in harmony with those heretofore known.
Always I was sensible of progress in him; a characteristic—as, I believe,
has been said in the foregoing pages—more perceptible in Franklin

Pierce than in any other person with whom I have been acquainted. He widened, deepened, rose to a higher point, and thus ever made himself equal to the ever-heightening occasion. This peculiarity of intellectual growth, continued beyond the ordinary period, has its analogy in his physical constitution—it being a fact that he continued to grow in stature between his twenty-first and twenty-fifth years.

He had not met with that misfortune, which, it is to be feared, befalls many men who throw their ardor into politics. The pursuit had taken nothing from the frankness of his nature; now, as ever, he used direct means to gain honorable ends; and his subtlety—for, after all, his heart and purpose were not such as he that runs may read—had the depth of wisdom, and never any quality of cunning. In great part, this undeteriorated manhood was due to his original nobility of nature. Yet it may not be unjust to attribute it, in some degree, to the singular good fortune of his life. He had never, in all his career, found it necessary to stoop. Office had sought him; he had not begged it nor manoeuvred for it, nor crept towards it—arts which too frequently bring a man, morally bowed and degraded, to a position which should be one of dignity, but in which he will vainly essay to stand upright.

In our earlier meetings, after Pierce had begun to come forward in public life, I could discern that his ambition was aroused. He felt a young man's enjoyment of success, so early and so distinguished. But as years went on, such motive seemed to be less influential with him. He was cured of ambition, as, one after another, its objects came to him unsought. His domestic position likewise, had contributed to direct his tastes and wishes towards the pursuits of private life. In 1834, he had married Jane Means, a daughter of the Rev. Dr. Appleton, a former president of Bowdoin College. Three sons, the first of whom died in early infancy, were born to him; and, having hitherto been kept poor by his public service, he no doubt became sensible of the expediency of making some provision for the future. Such, it may be presumed, were the considerations that induced his resignation of the senatorship, greatly to the regret of all parties. The senators gathered around him as he was about to quit the chamber; political opponents took leave of him as of a personal friend and no departing member has ever retired from that dignified body amid warmer wishes for his happiness than those that attended Franklin Pierce.

His father had died three years before, in 1839, at the mansion which he built, after the original log cabin grew too narrow for his rising family and fortunes. The mansion was spacious, as the liberal hospitality of the occupant required, and stood on a little eminence, surrounded by verdure and abundance, and a happy population, where, half a century before, the revolutionary soldier had come alone into the wilderness, and levelled the primeval forest trees. After being spared to behold the distinction of his son, he departed this life at the age of eighty-one years, in perfect peace, and, until within a few hours of his death, in the full possession of his intellectual powers. His last act was one of charity to a poor neighbor—a fitting close to a life that had abounded in such deeds. Governor Pierce was a man of admirable qualities—brave, active, public-spirited, endowed with natural authority, courteous yet simple in his manners; and in his son we may perceive these same attributes, modified and softened by a finer texture of character, illuminated by higher intellectual culture, and polished by a larger intercourse with the world, but as substantial and sterling as in the good old patriot.

Franklin Pierce had removed from Hillsborough in 1838, and taken up his residence at Concord, the capital of New Hampshire. On this occasion, the citizens of his native town invited him to a public dinner, in token of their affection and respect. In accordance with his usual taste, he gratefully accepted the kindly sentiment but declined the public demonstration of it.

3

HIS SUCCESS AT THE BAR

FRANKLIN PIERCE'S earliest effort at the bar, as we have already observed, was an unsuccessful one; but instead of discouraging him, the failure had only served to awaken the consciousness of latent power, and the resolution to bring it out. Since those days, he had indeed gained reputation as a lawyer. So much, however, was the tenor of his legal life broken up by the months of public service subtracted from each year, and such was the inevitable tendency of his thoughts towards political subjects, that he could but very partially avail himself of the opportunities of professional advancement. But on retiring from the Senate, he appears to have started immediately into full practice. Though the people of New Hampshire already knew him well, yet his brilliant achievements as an advocate brought him more into their view, and into closer relations with them, than he had ever before been. He now met his countrymen, as represented in the jury box, face to face, and made them feel what manner of man he was. Their sentiment towards him soon grew to be nothing short of enthusiasm; love, pride, the sense of brotherhood, affectionate sympathy, and perfect trust, mingled in it. It was the influence of a great heart pervading the general heart, and throbbing with in the same pulsation.

It has never been the writer's good fortune to listen to one of Franklin Pierce's public speeches, whether at the bar or elsewhere; nor, by diligent inquiry, has he been able to gain a very definite idea of the mode in which he produces his effects. To me, therefore, his foren-

28

sic displays are in the same category with those of Patrick Henry, or any other orator whose tongue, beyond the memory of man, has mouldered into dust. His power results, no doubt, in great measure, from the earnestness with which be imbues himself with the conception of his client's cause; insomuch that be makes it entirely his own, and, never undertaking a case which he believes to be unjust, contends with his whole heart and conscience, as well as intellectual force, for victory. His labor in the preparation of his cases is said to be unremitting; and he throws himself with such energy into a trial of importance, as wholly to exhaust his strength.

Few lawyers, probably, have been interested in a wider variety of business than he; its scope comprehends the great causes where immense pecuniary interests are concerned—from which, however, he is always ready to turn aside, to defend the humble rights of the poor man, or give his protection to one unjustly accused.

As one of my correspondents observes, "When an applicant has interested him by a recital of oppression, fraud, or wrong, General Pierce never investigates the man's estate before engaging in his business; neither does he calculate whose path he may cross. I have been privy to several instances of the noblest independence on his part, in pursuing, to the disrepute of those who stood well in the community, the weal of an obscure client with a good cause."

In the practice of the law, as Pierce pursued it, in one or another of the court houses of New Hampshire, the rumor of each successive struggle and success resounded over the rugged hills, and perished without a record. Those mighty efforts, into which he put all his strength, before a county court, and addressing a jury of yeomen, have necessarily been, as regards the evanescent memory of any particular trial, like the eloquence that is sometimes poured out in a dream. In other spheres of action, with no greater expenditure of mental energy, words have been spoken that endure from age to age— deeds done that harden into history. But this, perhaps the most earnest portion of Franklin Pierce's life, has left few materials from which it can be written. There is before me only one report of a case in which he was engaged—the defence of the Wentworths, at a preliminary examination, on a charge of murder. His speech occupied four hours in the delivery, and handles a confused medley of facts with masterly skill, bringing them to bear one upon another, and making the entire mass, as it were, transparent, so that the truth may be seen through it. The whole hangs together too closely to permit the quotation of passages.

The writer has been favored with communications from two individuals, who have enjoyed the best of opportunities to become acquainted with General Pierce's character as a lawyer. The following is the graceful and generous tribute of a gentleman, who, of late, more frequently than any other, has been opposed to him, at the bar:—

"General Pierce cannot be said to have commenced his career at the bar, in earnest, until after his resignation of the office of senator, in 1842. And it is a convincing proof of his eminent powers, that he at once placed himself in the very first rank at a bar so distinguished for ability as that of New Hampshire. It is confessed by all, who have the means of knowledge and judgment on this subject, that in no state of the Union are causes tried with more industry of preparation, skill, perseverance, energy, or vehement effort to succeed.

"During much of this time, my practice in our courts was suspended; and it is only within three or four years that I have had opportunities of intimately knowing his powers as an advocate, by being associated with him at the bar; and, most of all, of appreciating and feeling that power, by being opposed to him in the trial of causes before juries. Far more than any other man, whom it has been my fortune to meet, he makes himself felt by one who tries a case against him. From the first, he impresses on his opponent a consciousness of the necessity of a deadly struggle, not only in order to win the victory, but to avoid defeat.

"His vigilance and perseverance, omitting nothing in the preparation and introduction of testimony, even to the minutest details, which can be useful to his clients; his watchful attention, seizing on every weak point in the opposite case; his quickness and readiness; his sound and excellent judgment; his keen insight into character and motives, his almost intuitive knowledge of men; his ingenious and powerful cross examinations; his adroitness in turning aside troublesome testimony, and availing himself of every favorable point; his quick sense of the ridiculous; his pathetic appeals to the feelings; his sustained eloquence, and remarkable energetic declamation,—all mark him for a 'leader.'

"From the beginning to the end of the trial of a case, nothing with him is neglected, which can by possibility honorably conduce to success. His manner is always respectful and deferential to the court, captivating to the jury, and calculated to conciliate the good will even of those who would be otherwise indifferent spectators. In short, he plays the part of a successful actor; successful, because he always identifies himself with his part, and in him it is not acting.

"Perhaps, as would be expected by those who know his generosity of heart, and his scorn of every thing like oppression or extortion, he is most powerful in his indignant denunciations of fraud or injustice, and his addresses to the feelings in behalf of the poor and lowly, and the sufferers under wrong. I remember to have heard of his extraordinary power on one occasion, when a person, who had offered to procure arrears of a pension for revolutionary services, had appropriated to himself a most unreasonable share of the money. General Pierce spoke of the frequency of these instances, and, before the numerous audience, offered his aid, freely and gratuitously, to redress the wrongs of a widow or representative of a revolutionary officer or soldier, who had been made the subject of such extortion.

"The reply of the poor man, in the anecdote related by Lord Campbell, of Harry Erskine, would be applicable, as exhibiting a feeling to kindred that with which General Pierce is regarded: 'There's no a puir man in a' Scotland need to want a friend or fear an enemy, sae lang as Harry Erskine lives!'"

We next give his aspect as seen from the bench in the following carefully-prepared and discriminating article, from the chief justice of New Hampshire:—

"In attempting to estimate the character and qualifications of Mr. Pierce as a lawyer and an advocate, we undertake a delicate, but, at the same time, an agreeable task. The profession of the law, practised by men of liberal and enlightened minds, and unstained by the sordidness which more or less affects all human pursuits, invariably confers honor upon, and is honored by its followers. An integrity above suspicion, an eloquence alike vigorous and persuasive, and an intuitive sagacity have earned for Mr. Pierce the reputation that always follows them.

"The last case of paramount importance in which he was engaged as counsel was that of Morrison v. Philbrick, tried in the month of February, 1852, at the Court of Common Pleas for the county of Belknap. There was on both sides an array of eminent professional talent, Messrs. Pierce, Bell, and Bellows appearing for the defendant, and Messrs. Atherton and Whipple for the plaintiff. The case was one of almost unequalled interest to the public generally, and to the inhabitants of the country lying around the lower part of Lake Winnipesogee. A company, commonly called the Lake Company, had become the owners of many of the outlets of the streams supplying the lake, and by means of their works at such places, and at Union Bridge, a few miles below, were enabled to keep back the waters of the lake, and to use them, as occasion should require, to supply the mills at Lowell. The plaintiff alleged that the dam at Union Bridge had caused the water to rise higher than was done by the dam that existed in the year 1828, and that he was essentially injured thereby. The case had been on trial nearly seven weeks. Evidence equivalent to the testimony of one hundred and eighty witnesses had been laid before the jury. Upon this immense mass of facts, involving a great number of issues, Mr. Pierce was to meet his most formidable opponent in the state, Mr. Atherton. In that gentleman are united many of the rarest qualifications of an advocate. Of inimitable self-possession; with a coolness and clearness of intellect which no sudden emergencies can disturb; with that confidence in his resources which nothing but native strength, aided by the most thorough training, can bestow; with a felicity and fertility of illustration, the result alike of an exquisite natural taste and a cultivation of those studies which refine while they strengthen the mind for forensic contests,— Mr. Atherton's argument was listened to with an earnestness and interest which showed the conviction of his audience that no ordinary man was addressing them.

"No one who witnessed that memorable trial will soon forget the argument of Mr. Pierce on that occasion. He was the counsel for the defendant, and was therefore to precede Mr. Atherton. He was to analyze and unfold to the jury this vast body of evidence under the watchful eyes of an opponent at once enterprising and cautious, and before whom it was necessary to be both bold and skilful. He was to place himself in the position of the jury, to see the evidence as they would be likely to regard it, to understand the character of their minds, and what views would be the most likely to impress them. He was not only to be familiar with his own case, but to anticipate that of his opponent, and answer as he best might the argument of the counsel. And most admirably did he discharge the duties he had assumed on behalf of his client. Eminently graceful and attractive in his manner at all times, his demeanor was then precisely what it should have been, showing a manly confidence in himself and his case, and a courteous deference to the tribunal he was addressing. His erect and manly figure, his easy and unembarrassed air, bespoke the favorable attention of his audience. His earnest devotion to his cause, his deep emotion, evidently suppressed, but for that very reason all the more interesting, diffused themselves like electricity through his hearers. And when, as often happened, in the course of his argument, his

clear and musical accents fell upon the ear in eloquent and
pointed sentences, gratifying the taste while they satisfied the
reason, no man could avoid turning to his neighbor, and
expressing by his looks that pleasure which the very depth of
his interest forbade him to express in words. And when the
long trial was over, every one remembered with satisfaction
that these two distinguished gentlemen had met each other
during a most exciting and exhausting trial of seven weeks,
and that no unkind words, or captious passages, had occurred
between them, to diminish their mutual respect, or that in
which they were held by their fellow-citizens.

"In the above remarks, we have indicated a few of Mr.
Pierce's characteristics as an advocate; but he possesses other
endowments, to which we have not alluded. In the first place,
as he is a perfectly fearless man, so he is a perfectly fearless
advocate; and true courage is as necessary to the civilian as to
the soldier, and smiles and frowns Mr. Pierce disregards alike
in the undaunted discharge of his duty. He never fears to
uphold his client, how ever unpopular his cause may seem to
be for the moment. It is this courage which kindles his eloquence, inspires his conduct, and gives direction and firmness
to his skill. This it is which impels him onward, at all risks, to
lay bare every 'mystery of iniquity' which he believes is threat-
ening his case. He does not ask himself whether his opponent
be not a man of wealth and influence, of whom it might be
for his interest to speak with care and circumspection, but he
devotes himself with a ready zeal to his cause, careless of
aught but how he may best discharge his duty. His argumen-
tative powers are of the highest order. He never takes before
the court a position which he believes untenable. He has a
quick and sure perception of his points, and the power of
enforcing them by apt and pertinent illustrations. He sees the
relative importance and weight of different views, and can
assign to each its proper place, and brings forward the main
body of his reasoning in prominent relief, without distracting

the attention by unimportant particulars. And above all, he has the good sense, so rarely shown by many, to stop when he has said all that is necessary for the elucidation of his subject. With a proper confidence in his own perceptions, he states his views so pertinently, and in such precise and logical terms, that they cannot but be felt and appreciated. He never mystifies; he never attempts to pervert words from their proper and legitimate meaning, to answer a temporary purpose.

"His demeanor at the bar may be pronounced faultless. His courtesy in the court house, like his courtesy elsewhere, is that which springs from self-respect, and from a kindly heart, disposing its owner to say and do kindly things. But he would be a courageous man, who, presuming upon the affability of Mr. Pierce's manner, would venture a second time to attack him; for he would long remember the rebuke that followed his first attack. There is a ready repartee and a quick and cutting sarcasm in his manner when he chooses to display it, which it requires a man of considerable nerve to withstand. He is peculiarly happy in the examination of witnesses—that art in which so few excel. He never browbeats, he never attempts to terrify. He is never rude or discourteous. But the equivocating witness soon discovers that his falsehood is hunted out of its recesses with an unsparing determination. If he is dogged and surly, he is met by a spirit as resolute as his own. If he is smooth and plausible, the veil is lifted from him by a firm but graceful hand. If he is pompous and vain, no ridicule was ever more perfect than that to which he listens with astonished and mortified ears.

"The eloquence of Mr. Pierce is of a character not to be easily forgotten. He understands men, their passions, and their feelings. He knows the way to their hearts, and can make them vibrate to his touch. His language always attracts the hearer. A graceful and manly carriage, bespeaking him at once the gentleman and the true man, a manner warmed by the ardent glow of an earnest belief, an enunciation ringing, dis-

tinct, and impressive beyond that of most men, a command
of brilliant and expressive language, and an accurate taste,
together with a sagacious and instinctive insight into the
points of his case, are the secrets of his success. It is thus that
audiences are moved, and truth ascertained; and he will ever
be the most successful advocate who can approach the nearest to this lofty and difficult position.

"Mr. Pierce's views as a constitutional lawyer are such as
have been advocated by the ablest minds of America. They are
those which, taking their rise in the heroic age of the country,
were transmitted to him by a noble father, worthy of the
times in which he lived, worthy of that revolution which he
assisted in bringing about. He believe that the constitution
was made, not to be subverted, but to be sacredly preserved;
that a republic is perfectly consistent with the conservation of
law, of rational submission to right authority, and of true self-
government. Equally removed from that malignant hostility
to order which characterizes the demagogues who are eager
to rise upon the ruins even of freedom, and from that barren
and bigoted narrowness which would oppose all rational
freedom of opinion, he is, in its loftiest and most ennobling
sense, a friend of that Union, without which the honored
name of American citizen would become a by-word among
the nations. And if, as we fervently pray and confidently
expect he will, Mr. Pierce shall display before the great tri-
bunals of the nation the courage, the consistency, the sagacity, and the sense of honor, which have already secured for
him so many thousands of devoted friends, and which have
signalized both his private and professional life, his administration will long be held in grateful remembrance as one of
which the sense of right and the sagacity to perceive it, a clear
insight into the true destinies of the country, and a determination to uphold them at whatever sacrifice, were the pre-
dominant characteristics."

It may appear singular that Franklin Pierce has not taken up his residence in some metropolis, where his great forensic abilities would so readily find a more conspicuous theatre, and a far richer remuneration than heretofore. He himself, it is understood, has sometimes contemplated a removal, and, two or three years since, had almost determined on settling in Baltimore. But his native state, where he is known so well, and regarded with so much familiar affection, which be has served so faithfully, and which rewards him so generously with its confidence, New Hampshire, with its granite hills, must always be his home. He will dwell there, except when public duty, for a season, shall summon him away; he will die there, and give his dust to its soil.

It was at his option, in 1846, to accept the highest legal position in the country, setting aside the bench, and the one which, undoubtedly, would most have gratified his professional aspirations. President Polk, with whom he had been associated on the most friendly terms in Congress, now offered him the post of attorney general of the United States. "In tendering to you this position in my cabinet," writes the president, "I have been governed by the high estimate which I place upon your character and eminent qualifications to fill it. " The letter, in which this proposal is declined, shows so much of the writer's real self that we quote a portion of it.

> "Although the early years of my manhood were devoted to public life, it was never really suited to my taste. I longed, as I am sure you must often have done, for the quiet and independence that belong only to the private citizen; and now, at forty, I feel that desire stronger than ever.
>
> "Coming so unexpectedly as this offer does, it would be difficult, if not impossible, to arrange the business of an extensive practice, between this and the first of November, in a manner at all satisfactory to myself, or to those who have committed their interests to my care, and who rely on my services. Besides, you know that Mrs. Pierce's health, while at Washington, was very delicate. It is, I fear, even more so now; and the responsibilities which the proposed change would

necessarily impose upon her ought, probably, in themselves, to constitute an insurmountable objection to leaving our quiet home for a public station at Washington.

"When I resigned my seat in the Senate in 1842, I did it with the fixed purpose never again to be voluntarily separated from my family for any considerable length of time, except at the call of my country in time of war; and yet this consequence, for the reason before stated, and on account of climate, would be very likely to result from my acceptance.

"These are some of the considerations which have influenced my decision. You will, I am sure, appreciate my motives. You will not believe that I have weighed my personal convenience and ease against the public interest, especially as the office is one which, if not sought, would be readily accepted by gentlemen who could bring to your attainments and qualifications vastly superior to mine."

Previous to the offer of the attorney generalship, the appointment of United States senator had been tendered to Pierce by Governor Steele, and declined. It is unquestionable that, at this period, he hoped and expected to spend a life of professional toil in a private station, undistinguished except by exercise of his great talents in peaceful pursuits. But such was not his destiny. The contingency to which he referred in the above letter, as the sole exception to his purpose of never being separated from his family, was now about to occur. Nor did he fail to comport himself as not only that intimation, but the whole tenor of his character, gave reason to anticipate.

During the years embraced in this chapter,— between 1842 and 1847,—he had constantly taken an efficient interest in the politics of the state, but had uniformly declined the honors which New Hampshire was at all times ready to confer upon him. A democratic convention nominated him governor, but could not obtain his acquiescence. One of the occasions on which he most strenuously exerted himself was in holding the democratic party loyal to its principles, in opposition to the course of John P. Hale. This gentleman, then a rep-

resentative in Congress, had broken with his party on no less important a point than the annexation of Texas. He has never since acted
with the democracy, and has long been a leader of the free soil party.

In 1844 died Frank Robert, son of Franklin Pierce, aged four
years, a little boy of rare beauty and promise, and whose death was the
greatest affliction that his father has experienced. His only surviving
child is a son, now eleven years old

An engraving of Benjamin Pierce, father of Franklin, from a painting done when he was Governor of New Hampshire. (NHHS)

An engraving of Pierce done from a likeness painted during his Presidency.
Courtesy New Hampshire Historical Society (NHHS)

The Franklin Pierce Homestead in Hillsboro, N.H., circa 1900 from a postcard. Pierce was born nearby and grew up in this building.(NHHS)

An interior view of the Pierce Homestead showing some of the original decor. (NHHS)

Jane Means Appleton Pierce, circa 1850. (NHHS)

A campaign poster from 1851 depicting the Democratic Ticket, General Franklin Pierce and William S. King. (NHHS)

A derogatory political cartoon of Pierce kissing the ground at the devil's feet circulated by his opponents during the presidential campaign. (NHHS)

The Pierce's beloved son, "Benny," in a locket which belonged to Mrs. Pierce. (NHHS).

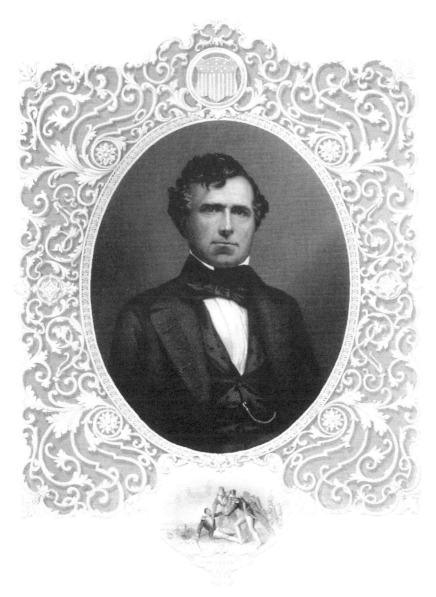

An engraving done during the Pierce Administration. (NHHS)

Jane Pierce showing the strain and grief she experienced during her husband's term as president. (NHHS)

Franklin Pierce at the end of his term as president. (NHHS)

Heroic portrait of "Gen. Franklin Pierce," showing Pierce in Mexico during the war, designed and engraved on steel by W. L. Ormsby, N.Y.

4

THE MEXICAN WAR—
HIS JOURNAL OF THE MARCH
FROM VERA CRUZ

WHEN FRANKLIN PIERCE declined the honorable offer of the attorney generalship of the United States, he intimated that there might be one contingency in which he would feel it his duty to give up the cherished purpose of spending the remainder of his life in a private station. That exceptional case was brought about, in 1847, by the Mexican war. He showed his readiness to redeem the pledge by enrolling himself as the earliest volunteer of a company raised in Concord, and went through the regular drill, with his fellow-soldiers, as a private in the ranks. On the passage of the bill for the increase of the army, be received the appointment of colonel of the Ninth Regiment, which was the quota of New England towards the ten that were to be raised. And shortly afterwards,—in March, 1847,—he was commissioned as brigadier general in the army; his brigade consisting of regiments from the extreme north, the extreme west, and the extreme south of the Union.

There is nothing in any other country similar to what we see in our own, when the blast of the trumpet at once converts men of peaceful pursuits into warriors. Every war in which America has been engaged has done this; the valor that wins our battles is not the trained hardihood of veterans, but a native and spontaneous fire; and there is surely a chivalrous beauty in the devotion of the citizen soldier to his country's cause, which the man who makes arms his profession, and is but doing his regular business on the field of battle, cannot pretend to rival. Taking the Mexican war as a specimen, this peculiar composition of an American army, as well in respect to its officers as its private soldiers, seems to create a spirit of romantic adventure which more than supplies the place of disciplined courage.

The author saw General Pierce, in Boston, on the eve of his departure for Vera Cruz. He had been intensely occupied, since his appointment, in effecting the arrangements necessary on leaving his affairs, as well as by the preparations, military and personal, demanded by the expedition. The transports were waiting at Newport to receive the troops. He was now in the midst of bustle, with some of the officers of his command about him, mingled with the friends whom he was to leave behind. The severest point of the crisis was over, for he had already bidden his family farewell. His spirits appeared to have risen with the occasion. He was evidently in his element; nor, to say the truth, dangerous as was the path before him, could it be regretted that his life was now to have the opportunity of that species of success which—in his youth, at least—he had considered the best worth struggling for. He looked so fit to be a soldier, that it was impossible to doubt—not merely his good conduct, which was as certain before the event as afterwards, but—his good fortune in the field, and his fortunate return.

He sailed from Newport on the 27th of May, in the bark *Kepler*, having on board three companies of the Ninth Regiment of Infantry, together with Colonel Ransom, its commander, and the officers belonging to the detachment. The passage was long and tedious, with protracted calms, and so smooth a sea that a sail boat might have performed the voyage in safety. The *Kepler* arrived at Vera Cruz in precisely a month after her departure from the United States, without speaking a single vessel from the south during the passage, and, of course, receiving no intelligence as to the position and state of the army which these reenforcements were to join.

From a journal kept by General Pierce, and intended only for the perusal of his family and friends, we present some extracts. They are mere hasty jottings-down in camp, and at the interval of weary marches, but will doubtless bring the reader closer to the man than any narrative which we could substitute.

"*June 28*. The vomito rages fearfully; and the city every where appears like the very habitation of pestilence. I have ordered the troops to be taken directly from the transports to Virgara, a extensive sand beach upon the gulf, where there is already an encampment consisting of four or five hundred men, under the command of Major Lally. The officers are under much apprehension on account of the climate and the vomito, the statements with regard to which are perhaps exaggerated. My orders are to make no delay here, and yet there is no preparation for my departure. About two thousand wild mules had been collected; but through the carelessness of persons employed by the quartermaster's department, (a precious set of scoundrels, it being possible to obtain few but desperate characters to enter this service here at this season,) a stampede has occurred to-day, by which fifteen hundred have been lost. The Mexicans fully believe that most of my command must die of vomito before I can be prepared to march into the interior.

"*July 5*. Pitched my tent at Virgara, two miles from the city. Mornings close, and heat excessive. Fine breeze after eleven o'clock, with breakers dashing upon the smooth beach for three miles. Our tents are upon the sand, which is as hard as the beach at Lynn or Hampton. Heavy rains, and tremendous thunder, and the most vivid and continuous flashes of lightning, almost every night. Many of the officers and soldiers are indisposed; but as yet there is no clear case of vomito. The troops are under drill every morning, the sun being too intense and oppressive to risk exposure at any other period of the day. I find my tent upon the beach decidedly preferable to any quarters in the city. Neither officers nor soldiers are allowed to go to the city except by special permission, and on duty.

"*July 6*. Mules and mustangs are being collected daily; but they are wild, unaccustomed to the harness, and most of them even to the bridle. Details from the different commands are actively engaged in taming these wild animals, and breaking them to harness.

"*July 7*. Last night, at ten o'clock, there was a stampede, as it is called in camp. The report of musketry at the advanced picket induced me to order the long roll to be beaten, and the whole command was at once formed in line of battle. I proceeded in person, with two companies, to the advanced picket, and found no ground for the alarm, although the sentinels insisted that a party of guerillas had approached within gun shot of their posts. I have ordered that, upon the repetition of any such alarm, the two companies nearest the picket shall proceed at once to the advanced post. The long roll will not be beaten until a report shall be sent in from the commanding officer of the detachment, who is to take with him a small detachment of cavalry as couriers. This will secure the quiet of the camp at night, and at the same time afford protection against surprise.

"*July 8*. Lieutenant T. J. Whipple, adjutant of the Ninth Infantry, was induced by curiosity to visit, with private Barnes of Manchester, the cemetery near the wall of the city—an imprudent act, especially as the audacity of the guerillas, and their daily near approach, have been well understood. That he should have gone with a single unarmed private, and himself without arms except his sabre, is astonishing. Lieutenant Whipple was attacked by six guerillas, and overpowered. Barnes escaped, and found me, within half an hour, at Governor Wilson's quarters. I immediately despatched a troop of cavalry in pursuit; but no trace of the miscreants has been discovered, and great alarm is felt for the safety of our gallant, but too adventurous, friend. There was in my command no braver man or better soldier than Whipple.

"*July 12*. Being informed that Adjutant Whipple's life had been spared, and that he was a prisoner with a band of guerillas about twelve or fourteen miles from my camp, I sent a strong detachment, by night, to surprise the ranchero, and, if possible, to recover our valued friend. The village was taken, but the guerillas had fled with their prisoner. Captain Duff, the efficient and gallant commander of cavalry, attached to my command, having been greatly exposed in an excursion in search of Whipple, is dangerously sick of vomito.

"About eighty American horses have reached me from New Orleans, and I shall put my command in motion to-morrow or the next day. I know not how long my delay might have continued, but for the activity of my officers generally, and especially if I had not secured the services of a most efficient staff, which has cheerfully rendered its aid in season and out of season. Major Woods, of the Fifteenth Infantry, a graduate of West Point, and an officer of great intelligence, experience, and coolness, kindly consented to act as my adjutant general. My aid-de-camp, Lieutenant Thom, of the Topographical Engineers, Lieutenant Caldwell, of the Marine Corps, brigade commissary, and Lieutenant Van Bocklin, of the Seventh Infantry, brigade quartermaster, have all, regardless of the dangers of the climate, performed an amount of labor, in pushing forward the preparations for our march, which entitles them not merely to my thanks, but to a substantial acknowledgment from government. Major Lally is dangerously sick of vomito. I have sent him in an ambulance, on my mattress, to Major Smith's quarters, in the city, to-day. Major Seymour is also sick, but is determined to go on with the command. I visited the gallant Captain Duff this morning, and have decided to send him to the hospital, in the city. His is an undoubted case of the vomito, and I fear that but slight hope of his recovery can be reasonably indulged. I feel his loss seriously; he was a truly brave and efficient officer.

"*July 13.* After a delay of nearly three weeks, in this debilitating and sickly climate, where I had reason to expect, before landing, a delay of not more than two days,—and after an amount of labor and perplexity more trying than an active campaign in the field,—the hum and clank of preparation, the strand covered with wagons, going to and returning from the city, laden with ammunition, subsistence, &c., sufficiently indicate that the long-deferred movement is at last to be made.

"*July 14.* Colonel Ransom, with the Ninth Infantry, and two companies of the Twelfth, under Captain Wood, left this morning, with about eighty wagons of the train. He will proceed to San Juan, twelve miles distant, on the Jalapa road, and there await my arrival with the remainder of the brigade. It would be almost certain destruction to men and teams, so long as we remain in tierra caliente, to march them between the hours of nine o'clock, A. M., and four, P. M. Colonel Ransom's command, therefore, struck their tents last night, loaded their company wagons, and bivouacked, in order that there might be nothing to delay an early start in the morning. Fortunately, it did not rain, and the advance moved off in fine order and spirits.

"*July 15.* It is impossible for me to move today, with the remainder of the brigade, on account of the deficiency of teams. Notwithstanding all my exertions, I shall be compelled to rely on many mule teams, which, when I move, will be in harness for the first time. I have, however, sent off a second detachment, consisting of four companies of the Fourteenth and two companies of the Third Infantry, under the command of that accomplished and admirable officer, Lieutenant Colonel Hebert, of Louisiana.

"*July 16.* After much perplexity and delay, on account of the unbroken and intractable teams, I left the camp, this afternoon, at five o'clock, with the Fourth Artillery, Lieutenant Colonel Watson's Marine Corps, and a detachment of the Third Dragoons, with about forty wagons. The road was very heavy; the wheels sinking almost to the hubs in sand, and the untried and untamed teams almost constantly bolting, in some part of the train. We were occupied rather in breaking the animals to harness, than in performing a march. At ten o'clock at night, we bivouacked, in the darkness and sand, by the wagons in the road—having made but three miles from camp.

"*Camp near San Juan, July 17.* Started this morning, at four o'clock. Road still heavy, over short, steep hills; progress slow and difficult. Reached Santa Fe, eight miles from Vera Cruz, at eight o'clock, A. M. Heat exceedingly oppressive. Remained here till four, P. M. About twelve o'clock, two mule-teers came to our bivouac in great agitation, to announce that five hundred guerillas were on the Jalapa road, not five hundred yards distant, advancing rapidly. Lieutenant Colonel Watson, with the Marine Corps, is, by order, immediately under arms, and Major Gavet, with two pieces of artillery, in position to keep the road. No guerilla force approaches; and it is doubtful whether the muleteers, looking through the medium of terror, were not entirely mistaken. Still, it was our first alarm, and useful, as stimulating to vigilance and constant preparation for an attack.

"Resumed the march at four P. M., and reached San Juan about nine o'clock in the evening, in a drenching rain. The road from Santa Fe to this place is level and firm; no water, until the first branch of the San Juan is reached. The guerillas had attempted to destroy the bridge over the stream; but Colonel Ransom's advance was upon them before the work of destruction was complete, and New England strength and ingenuity readily repaired damages. The rain continued to pour, throughout that night, the next day, and the night following. The encampment being upon low, muddy ground, along the margin of the stream, officers and men were compelled to find their only repose, literally, in the mud and water; and I resolved to move, notwithstanding the heavy rain, which continued to pour until the evening of the 19th.

"*Telema Nueva, July 20.* My brigade, with the exception of Lieutenant Colonel Bonham's command, left Camp Pierce, (a name given it before my arrival, by Colonel Ransom,) at San Juan, yesterday evening, and marched to this place, twenty-four miles from Vera Cruz. Several escopettes were discharged upon the detachment of dragoons, at the head of the column.

These shots came from an eminence on the left of the road, a direct line to which was impracticable for cavalry. Lieutenant Deven, in command of the advanced detachment, dashed rapidly up the hill, along the road, to reconnoitre the position of the main body of the enemy, which, it was supposed, might be posted behind the eminence. Captain Ridgeley, of the Fourth Artillery, threw a few round shot in the direction from which the fire came; and in the mean time, I had despatched Captain Bodfish, of the Ninth Infantry, with the grenadiers and Company F., to take the enemy in flank. The duty was promptly and handsomely performed; but the enemy had fled before Captain B. had arrived within musket shot of his position.

"The march continued about a mile, when mounted Mexicans could be discerned at distant points, evidently reconnoitring. This being the place where Colonel Mcintosh's train had been attacked and sustained so much damage, I made dispositions for any such contingency. I detached Captain Larkin Smith, of the Eighth Infantry; with three companies of infantry and a party of dragoons, by a path on the left of the main road, that debouched from an old Spanish fort, whence an attack was anticipated. A detachment of dragoons under Lieutenant Deven, Colonel Ransom with the Ninth Infantry, and Captain Ridgeley with three pieces of his battery, marched on the main road. Captain Smith, having traversed the route upon which he was directed, again intersected the main road, near the fort above referred to, a little in advance of the head of our column.

"In this position, as soon as Captain Smith's detachment had well extended upon the road, the enemy opened a brisk fire. They were concealed and strongly posted in the chapperal, on both sides of the road—the greater number on the right. The fire was promptly returned, and sustained on both sides for some minutes, when Captain Ridgeley unlimbered one of his pieces, and threw a few canister shot among them. This immediately silenced the enemy's fire, which had been nearly done by Captain Smith, before the artillery came up. Captain Bodfish, with three companies of the Ninth Infantry, was sent to attack the enemy in flank; but his flight was too precipitous for this detachment to come up with his main body.

"I could not ascertain the enemy's loss. The Mexican paper at Jalapa stated it at forty; which, I think, was an exaggeration. Our own loss was six wounded, and seven horses shot.

"I witnessed with pleasure the conduct of that part of my command immediately engaged, on this occasion. The first fire of the enemy indicated a pretty formidable force, the precise strength of which could not be ascertained, as they were completely covered by the chapperal. It was the first time, on the march, that any portion of my command had been fairly under fire. I was at the head of the column, on the main road, and, witnessing the whole scene, saw nothing but coolness and courage on the part of both officers and men.

"*Puente Nacionale, July 21.* The brigade resumed its march yesterday, at three o'clock, and reached Paso de Orejas, three miles distant, where we encamped for the night. The march was unobstructed by the enemy; and our advanced troop reached the place last named at an early hour. The rear, however, in consequence of our immense train, did not arrive till after dark. As it descended towards the camp, it was approached by guerillas; but they were kept at bay by a few discharges from a six pounder, left with Lieutenant Colonel Watson, in the rear. These parties had been seen during the day, on distant and elevated points, reconnoitring our line. The road, on this part of the march, is high and dry; no water except in small ponds or pools. Paso de Orejas is on the west side of a rapid and beautiful stream, spanned by a substantial and expensive bridge; and, judging from the spacious buildings, it has evidently been a place of considerable business.

"We left Paso de Orejas at four o'clock in the morning, and

pursued our course uninterruptedly, until we reached Puente Nacionale. Anticipating, from rumors which had reached us upon the road, an attack at this place, and having no map of its defences, natural or artificial, I halted the entire command on the top of the long hill, which descends to the fork of the Antigua River. With a detail of two companies of the Twelfth Infantry, commanded by Captains Wood and Danvers, I proceeded in person, two or three hundred yards, to an elevation on the right of the road, from which, with my glass, I could command a view of the bridge, the village, and the enemy's positions. There were a few lancers in the village, riding rapidly from one position to another, flourishing a red flag, and occasionally, as if in defiance, coming up to the barricade which they had thrown across the bridge. The main body of the enemy, however, was posted behind a temporary breastwork on a bluff, a hundred and fifty feet high, commanding the whole bridge, and overhanging, as it were, the eastern arch. Their position could not be turned, as the heights continue precipitous from the water's edge, for a long distance below.

"The tongue of land, dividing the fork referred to above from the main stream of the Rio del Antigua, rises to an immense height on the left; and on this eminence is a fortification, which, from the road, has the appearance of great strength. After crossing the bridge, the road turns suddenly to the left. Having satisfied myself that this fort, on the left, was not occupied, I sent forward Captain Dobbins with his company, together with Company G, Fourth Infantry, and Company I, Voltigeurs, under Captain Archer, along the brow of the hill to the bank of the Antigua, opposite the village, with instructions, if possible, to cross the river above.

"The passage above, like that below, being found impracticable, I rode forward, with my aid-de-camp, Lieutenant Thom, to reconnoitre the enemy's works more closely, and to find on the left, if possible, a position for artillery. In this I was to a certain extent successful, and immediately ordered forward three pieces, two under the command of Captain Ridgeley, and one under Lieutenant Getty, of the Fourth Artillery. These were stationed on a piece of table land, perhaps an acre in extent, four or five rods from the west end of the main bridge, and thirty feet above it. The pieces swept the bridge, and dispersed the lancers from the village. Shots were also thrown at the heights, but, in consequence of the great elevation of the bluff where the enemy's main body were posted, without any other effect than to distract his fire from the advance, under Colonel Bonham, then awaiting my orders to cross. This portion of Colonel Bonham's command consisted of Company B, Twelfth Infantry, under Captain Holden, a detachment of the same regiment under Lieutenant Giles, two companies of Pennsylvania volunteers under Captains Caldwell and Taylor, Company C, Voltigeurs, under Lieutenant Forsyth, and Company F, Eleventh Infantry, commanded by Lieutenant Hedges.

"Under the discharge of the artillery of the enemy's works, the command was given to Colonel Bonham to advance. It was admirably executed. Captain Holden's company, leading, rushed over the bridge with a shout; the captain, some paces in advance, leaped the barricade of brush and timber, his men following with great enthusiasm. Having crossed the bridge, he threw his company, under the cover of buildings, immediately beneath the bluff, and taking a narrow, steep path to the right, was in a few moments upon the summit, where the whole brigade greeted him with hearty cheers. The remainder of the command followed rapidly, and in good order. In the mean time, with a view to cut off the retreat of the foe, Captain Dupreau, of the Third Dragoons, had leaped the barricade, dashed through the village, and, almost simultaneously with Captain Holden, planted the colors of his company upon the breastwork, from which the plunging fire had so recently ceased. The guerillas and lancers could hardly have waited, after the first shout of Holden's company, to see the effect of their own fire; for, before our first detachment reached their works, they were in full flight, beyond pursuit, in the dense chapperal of the mountains in their rear.

"Colonel Bonham's horse was shot near me, and I received an escopette hall through the rim of my hat, but without other damage than leaving my head, for a short time, without protection from the sun. The balls spattered like hailstones around us, at the moment the column advanced; and it seems truly wonderful that so few took effect. A large portion of them passed over our heads, and struck between the rear of Colonel Bonham's command and the main body of the brigade, two or three hundred yards behind, with the train; thus verifying what has so often been said by our gallant fellows, within the last forty days, that the nearer you get to these people in fight, the safer.

"The encampment was made in the village, for the night, thirty miles from Vera Cruz. Here General Santa Anna has a spacious and magnificent hacienda, in which I established my headquarters.

"*July 22.* I left the princely hacienda of Santa Anna, at the Natural Bridge, this morning at four o'clock. The moment our picket guards were withdrawn, the enemy appeared on all the surrounding heights, but at distances too respectful to provoke any particular notice. I proceeded on the march, without molestation, until we commenced the descent of the Plan del Rio, where Captain Dupreau's company of cavalry, a few hundred yards in front of the column, was fired upon from the chapperal, and three horses wounded. Lieutenant Colonel Hebert, being next to the dragoons, threw out a company of skirmishers on either side, and, with the remainder, continued the march on the main road. Nothing more, however, was seen or heard of the enemy.

"An old Spanish fort stands on a high eminence at the right of the road, commanding it in all directions, and overlooking the bridge. A bridge, about four hundred yards west of the main stream, had been barricaded, evidently with the intention of defending it. But neither the fort nor the position beyond the barricade was occupied; the enemy, as we soon learned, having hit upon another expedient for checking our advance, which they evidently believed must cause several weeks' detention, and probably drive the command back upon the coast.

"Removing the barricade at the small bridge, and proceeding about four hundred yards, we came to the Plan del Rio, over which there had been a bridge similar to Puente Nacionale. It was a magnificent structure of art, combining great strength and beauty, a work of the old Spaniards, so many of which are found upon this great avenue from the coast, fitted to awaken the admiration and wonder of the traveller. The fact that the main arch, a span of about sixty feet, had been blown up, first burst upon me as I stood upon the brink of the chasm, with a perpendicular descent of nearly a hundred feet to the bed of a rapid stream, much swollen by the recent rains. As far as the eye could reach, above and below, the banks on the west side, of vast height, descended precipitously, almost in a perpendicular line, to the water's edge.

"This sudden and unexpected barrier, I need not say, was somewhat withering to the confidence with which I had been animated. The news having extended back along the line, my officers soon crowded around me; and the deep silence that ensued was more significant than any thing which could have been spoken. After a few moment pause, this silence was broken by many short, epigrammatical remarks, and more questions. 'We have it before us now!' said Lieutenant Colonel Hebert. 'The destruction of this magnificent and expensive Work of a past generation could not have been ordered, but upon a deliberate and firm purpose of stern resistance.' 'This people have destroyed,' said another, 'what they never will rebuild.' 'What is to be done with this train?' 'What do you purpose now, general?' 'To have it closed up,' I replied, 'as

compactly as possible to-night, and to cross to-morrow with
every wagon!' But, I confess, there was no very distinct idea,
in my own mind, how the thing was to be accomplished.

"I ought to have mentioned that the Ninth Infantry,
under the gallant Colonel Ransom, which was that day in
advance, on discovering that the bridge had been blown up,
and supposing the enemy to be in force on the other side,
immediately descended the steep banks, by the aid of trees
and other supports, and forded the river. They then took possession of a church on the other side.

"A long hill descends from the west towards this river; the
road is narrow, and there is no ground for an encampment or
the packing of wagons. The wagons, therefore, having been
closed up, were of necessity left in the wood, making a line of
more than a mile and a half in length. Thus disposed, every
precaution was taken for the protection of the train, and the
brigade was left to bivouac.

"The growth, for miles around, was low and scrubby,
affording no timber to reconstruct the arch; and it was perfectly apparent that no passage could be effected at the north.
Lieutenant Thom, and two or three scientific officers with
him, had been occupied from the time of our arrival in making a careful reconnoissance down the banks of the river, for
two or three miles below. At dusk, they reported that the difficulties in that direction did not diminish, but that a road
might probably be constructed down the bank, some hundred yards south of the bridge. Weary, and not in the most
buoyant spirits, we all sunk to repose.

"Early the next morning, I sent for Captain Bodfish, of
the Ninth Infantry, an officer of high intelligence and force of
character. He had been engaged for many years in the lumber
business and accustomed to the construction of roads in the
wild and mountainous districts of Maine, and was withal a
man not lightly to be checked by slight obstacles in the
accomplishment of an enterprise. It occurred to me, there-

fore, that he was the very man whose services should, on this occasion, be put in requisition.

"Being informed of the object for which he had been called, he retired, and, returning in half a hour, said that he had examined the ground, and that the construction of a road, over which the train might safely pass, was practicable. 'What length of time,' he was asked, 'will necessarily be occupied in the completion of the work?' 'That,' said he, 'will depend upon the number of men employed. If you will give me five hundred men, I will furnish you a road over which the train can pass safely in four hours.' The detail was immediately furnished; and, at the end of three hours, this energetic and most deserving officer reported to me that the road was ready for the wagons. Fortune favored us in more respects than one. The water in the river, which, in the rainy season, is a rapid and unfordable stream, fell one and a half feet from the time of our arrival to the hour of the completion of the work. 'Bodfish's road' (unless this nation shall be regenerated) will be the road, at that place, for Mexican diligences, for half a century to come.

"Without removing an article from a single wagon, the entire train had passed, without accident, before the sun went down on the evening of the 23d. Here, on the east side of Plan del Rio, where there are barracks and many ranchos, we are comfortably quartered for the night. The troops are in the highest spirits; and jokes innumerable are passing among our southern brethren upon the absurdity of Mexicans attempting to play such a trick on Yankees. The heat had been so excessive that I intended to remain one day at this place, for the refreshment of men and animals; but all are anxious to proceed, and we move in the morning. Thus the destruction of this very expensive work, instead of retarding my progress for a single hour, has added fresh confidence and enthusiasm to the command.

"*Encero, July 24*. Plan del Rio being within four miles of

Cerro Gordo, and being apprehensive of a plunging fire on the trains, from the eminences, I despatched Lieutenant Colonel Bonham with five hundred picked men, at twelve o'clock, last night, to take possession of the heights, by the way of Twiggs's route, as it is called. An officer, in my command, was at the battle of Cerro Gordo, and supposed that he sufficiently understood the localities to act as guide. This military road of Twiggs turned off from the main road, four or five miles from Plan del Rio. I went forward in person, with Captain Dupreau's company of cavalry. The rain poured in torrents; and the darkness was such that I could not see Dupreau's white horse, while riding by his side. In consequence of this extreme darkness, Captain Scantland was unable to find the route, and I returned with the cavalry to camp. The detachment rested upon their arms till morning, when the duty was handsomely performed, although the strongholds were found unoccupied.

"When our train left Plan del Rio, at early dawn, the Mexicans appeared on the heights, and discharged a harmless volley upon the rear guard. They evidently made a mistake. Not having calculated distances with their usual accuracy, Colonel Ransom, being in the rear with a six pounder, under the command of Lieutenant Welsh, threw a few canister shot among them. These undoubtedly took effect, as they scattered in all directions without firing another gun. We reached this place at about two o'clock, where is another magnificent hacienda, owned by Santa Anna. There being large herds of cattle around us, but no owner of whom to purchase, I have sent out detachments to supply our immediate wants.

"Two or three of the young officers, desiring to participate in the chase of the cattle, left the camp without permission, and, in the excitement of the chase, wandered to a considerable distance. One of them has just been brought in with a dangerous gun shot through the thigh—a very natural result of such imprudence. The only matter of surprise is, that they were not all killed or captured by the hands of guerillas, who are known to hang upon our rear by day, and about our camp by night. I am sorry for the officer, but trust the admonition may be salutary. We have here a delightful encampment, upon a green carpet that slopes gently to a fine stream of clear, pure water. Jalapa is only eight miles distant.

"*Camp near Jalapa, July 25.* We left the encampment at Encero at seven o'clock, not without regret, so pleasant was the situation, and so refreshing the pure stream that rushed sparkling by us. It reminded all New England men of their homes. Our march to Jalapa, which we reached at noon, was uninterrupted. The main road to Puebla passes outside of the city. I rode with twenty dragoons to the principal fonda, kept by an intelligent Frenchman, where I dined, and remained two or three hours, until the train and rear of the command had passed. In the hotel, I met and conversed, through an interpreter, with many persons in the garb of gentlemen. Full of complimen ts and professions of friendship, they quite stagger a blunt Yankee. The truth is, instead of being induced to take up my quarters on account of these protestations, I the earlier thought it time, with my true friend and aid-de-camp, Lieutenant Thom, and the twenty dragoons, to join the command. I hardly know why, amid pleasant conversations, this feeling came over me. It was instinct, rather than any legitimate deduction from what I either saw or heard; but, in this case, it proved better than reason, for, returning to the main road, I found the extreme rear halted, and in no little excitement. A colored servant of Lieutenant Welsh, having been sent to water a horse, not six rods from the road, had been stabbed, and the horse stolen. I stopped long enough to ascertain that no trace could be found of the robbers, and then proceeded to camp, two and a half or three miles distant.

"The encampment is by a fine stream, which drives the spindles of Don Garcia, a quarter of a mile below us. This factory has in some respects a New England aspect, but is destitute of the indications of New England enterprise and thrift.

"No trust is to be placed in this people. I have learned, beyond a doubt, that Jalapa is daily filled with guerillas, and that many of these bravos were about the fonda, while we were there.

"*Camp near Jalapa, July 27.* Several soldiers, while strolling to the city or the neighboring ranchos, in violation of general orders, have, either deserted, been killed, or taken prisoners. Mr. N., a lawyer resident in New Orleans, but a native of Maine, having business in the interior of Mexico, was permitted to accompany my command from Vera Cruz. He seems to have been enjoying a stroll in the streets of Jalapa, when he was seized by the guerillas, who are evidently in disguise in all parts of the city. He wrote me a note after his capture, stating that he had been offered his liberty, if I would send to the Alcalde of Jalapa a certificate that he was a private citizen, and in no way connected with the American army. This was, of course, promptly forwarded.

"The guerillas, I believe, have complete possession, or rather control, of Jalapa. The citizens, who dread them more than we do, and who suffer severely from them, dare not inform against nor resist them, so long as an uncertainty exists with regard to protection from the American forces. They stroll about the city in disguise, and, whenever an opportunity presents itself, they kill or carry off our stragglers, and steal and rob with impunity.

"*Camp near La Hoya, July 29.* We left our camp near Jalapa this morning at seven o'clock. The sick list, instead of diminishing, has increased and now includes more than four hundred men. The principal cause is excessive indulgence in fruits, which it was found impossible to keep from the troops. We are now upon the margin of a stream, where are the remains of fires and other relics of a former encampment. The ground is low and level. The rain is pouring in torrents, and rushes through my tent, in a channel dug by the orderly, like a permanent, living brook.

"On arriving at San Miguel el Saldado, I required the Alcalde of that place, and another Mexican, to go forward with us as guides to the passes that turn the strong positions commanding the roads over which we shall pass to-morrow.

"Camp near the Castle of Perote, July 30. The whole command was under arms at dawn. Two regiments (the Ninth Infantry under Colonel Ransom, and detachments from various regiments under Lieutenant Colonel Bonham) were ordered to take the paths leading over the heights commanding the road, while the main body, with the train, should pass this strong defile. During the night, the Alcalde had furnished two guides, better acquainted with the paths than himself. One accompanied each of the flanking columns. This service, performed by Colonel Ransom and Lieutenant Colonel Bonham, was exceedingly arduous, although they occupied the heights without resistance. The train passed this gorge of the mountains, which furnishes the strongest natural defences, without molestation; the two flanking regiments making their appearance, every few moments, in the openings, and on the peaks of the surrounding summits.

"At Las Vegas, about four miles from Perote, we were met by Colonel Wyncoop, of the Pennsylvania volunteers, now in command of the castle, with Captain Walker's elegant company of mounted riflemen. Captain Walker is the same who gained (earned is the better word, for officers sometimes gain what they do not merit) such an enviable reputation on the Rio Grande. His company is in all respects worthy of their efficient, gentlemanly, modest, and daring commander.

"I reached the castle before dark, and Colonel Wyncoop kindly tendered me his quarters; but I adhered to a rule from which I have never deviated on the march—to see the rear of the command safely in camp, and where they pitched their tents to pitch my own. The rear guard, in consequence of the broken condition of the road, did not arrive until nine o'clock; when our tents were pitched in darkness, and in the sand, which surrounds the castle on all sides.

"*Camp under the Walls of the Castle of Perote, August 1.* We make a halt here of two or three days, to repair damages, procure supplies, and give rest to the troops. I have sent two hundred sick to the hospital in the castle, and received about the same number of convalescents, left by trains that have preceded me.

"While at the artillery quarters, to-day, in the village, Captain Ruff arrived, with his company of cavalry and the company of native spies, as they are called, now in our service, and commanded by the celebrated robber Domingues. Captain Ruff was sent forward by General Persifer F. Smith. The latter, in consequence of the rumors that had reached the commander-in-chief, in relation to the attacks made upon my command, had been sent down as far as Ojo del Agua, with a view to ascertain my whereabouts and condition, and to afford support, if necessary."

General Pierce's journal here terminates. In its clear and simple narrative, the reader cannot fail to see— although it was written with no purpose of displaying them—the native qualities of a born soldier, together with the sagacity of an experienced one. He had proved himself, moreover, physically apt for war, by his easy endurance of the fatigues of the march; every step of which (as was the case with few other officers) was performed either on horseback or on foot. Nature, indeed, has endowed him with a rare elasticity both of mind and body; he springs up from pressure like a well-tempered sword. After the severest toil, a single night's rest does as much for him, in the way of refreshment, as a week could do for most other men.

His conduct on this adventurous march received the high encomiums of military men, and was honored with the commendation of the great soldier who is now his rival in the presidential contest. He reached the main army at Puebla, on the 7th of August, with twenty-four hundred men, in fine order, and without the loss of a single wagon.

5

HIS SERVICES IN THE VALLEY OF MEXICO

GENERAL SCOTT, who was at Puebla with the main army, awaiting this reenforcement, began his march towards the city of Mexico on the day after General Pierce's arrival. The battle of Contreras was fought on the 19th of August.

The enemy's force consisted of about seven thousand men, posted in a strongly-intrenched camp, under General Valencia, one of the bravest and ablest of the Mexican commanders. The object of the commanding general appears to have been to cut off the communications of these detached troops with Santa Anna's main army, and thus to have them entirely at his mercy. For this purpose, a portion of the American forces were ordered to move against Valencia's left flank, and, by occupying strong positions in the villages and on the roads towards the city, to prevent reenforcements from reaching him. In the mean time, to draw the enemy's attention from this movement, a vigorous onset was made upon his front; and as the operations upon his flank were not immediately and fully carried out according to the plan, this front demonstration assumed the character of a fierce and desperate attack, upon which the fortunes of the day much depended. General Pierce's brigade formed a part of the force engaged in this latter movement, in which four thousand newly-recruited men, unable to bring their artillery to bear, contended against seven thousand disciplined soldiers, protected by intrenchments, and showering round shot and shells against the assailing troops.

The ground in front was of the rudest and roughest character. The troops made their way with difficulty over a broken tract, called the Pedregal, bristling with sharp points of rocks, and which is represented as having been the crater of a now exhausted and extinct volcano. The enemy had thrown out skirmishers, who were posted in great force among the crevices and inequalities of this broken ground, and vigorously resisted the American advance; while the artillery of the intrenched camp played upon our troops, and shattered the very rocks over which they were to pass.

General Pierce's immediate command had never before been under such a fire of artillery. The enemy's range was a little too high, or the havoc in our ranks must have been dreadful. In the midst of this fire, General Pierce, being the only officer mounted in the brigade, leaped his horse upon an abrupt eminence, and addressed the colonels and captains of the regiments, as they passed, in a few stirring words—reminding them of the honor of their country, of the victory their steady valor would contribute to achieve. Pressing forward to the head of the column, he had nearly reached the practicable ground that lay beyond, when his horse slipped among the rocks, thrust his foot into a crevice, and fell, breaking his own leg, and crushing his rider heavily beneath him.

Pierce's mounted orderly soon came to his assistance. The general was stunned, and almost insensible. When partially recovered, he found himself suffering from severe bruises, and especially from a sprain of the left knee, which was undermost when the horse came down. The orderly assisted him to reach the shelter of a projecting rock; and as they made their way thither, a shell fell close beside them, and exploded, covering them with earth. "That was a lucky miss," said Pierce calmly. Leaving him in such shelter as the rock afforded, the orderly went in search of aid, and was fortunate to meet with Dr. Ritchie, of Virginia, who was attached to Pierce's brigade, and was following in close proximity to the advancing column. The doctor administered to him as well as the circumstances would admit. Immediately on recovering his full consciousness, General Pierce had become anxious to rejoin his troops; and now, in opposition to Dr. Ritchie's advice and remonstrances, he determined to proceed to the front.

With pain and difficulty, and leaning on his orderly's arm, he reached the battery commanded by Captain McGruder, where he found the horse of Lieutenant Johnson, who had just before received a mortal wound. In compliance with his wishes, he was assisted into the saddle; and, in answer to a remark that he would be unable to keep his seat, "Then," said the general, "you must tie me on." Whether this precaution was actually taken is a point on which authorities differ; but at all events, with injuries so severe as would have sent almost any other man to the hospital, he rode forward into the battle.

The contest was kept up until nightfall, without forcing Valencia's intrenchment. General Pierce remained in the saddle until eleven o'clock at night. Finding himself, at nine o'clock, the senior officer in the field, he, in that capacity, withdrew the troops from their advanced position, and concentrated them at the point where they were to pass the night. At eleven, beneath a torrent of rain, destitute of a tent or other protection, and without food or refreshment, he lay down on an ammunition wagon, but was prevented by the pain of his injuries, especially that of his wounded knee, from finding any repose. At one o'clock came orders from General Scott to put the brigade into a new position, in front of the enemy's works, preparatory to taking part in the contemplated operations of the next morning. During the night, the troops appointed for that service, under Riley, Shields, Smith, and Cadwallader, had occupied the villages and roads between Valencia's position and the city; so that, with daylight, the commanding general's scheme of the battle was ready to be carried out, as it had originally existed in his mind

At daylight, accordingly, Valencia's entrenched camp was assaulted. General Pierce was soon in the saddle, at the head of his brigade, which retained its position in front, thus serving to attract the enemy's attention, and divert him from the true point of attack. The camp was stormed in the rear by the American troops, led on by Riley, Cadwallader, and Dimmick; and in the short space of seventeen minutes it had fallen into the hands of the assailants, together with a multitude of prisoners. The remnant of the routed enemy fled towards Churubusco. As Pierce led his brigade in pursuit, crossing the battle field, and passing through the works that had just been stormed, he found the road and adjacent fields every where strewn with the dead and dying. The pursuit was continued until one o'clock, when the foremost of the Americans arrived in front of the strong Mexican positions at Churubusco and San Antonio, where Santa Anna's army had been compelled to make a stand, and where the great conflict of the day commenced.

General Santa Anna entertained the design of withdrawing his forces towards the city. In order to intercept this movement, Pierce's brigade, with other troops, was ordered to pursue a route by which the enemy could be attacked in the rear. Colonel Noah E. Smith (a patriotic American, long resident in Mexico, whose local and topographical knowledge proved eminently serviceable) had offered to point out the road, and was sent to summon General Pierce to the presence of the commander-in-chief. When he met Pierce, near Coyacan, at the head of his brigade, the heavy fire of the batteries had commenced. "He was exceedingly thin," writes Colonel Smith, "worn down by the fatigue and pain of the day and night before, and then evidently suffering severely. Still, there was a glow in his eye, as the cannon boomed, that showed within him a spirit ready for the conflict." He rode up to General Scott, who was at this time sitting on horseback beneath a tree, near the church of Coyacan, issuing orders to different individuals of his staff. Our account of this interview is chiefly taken from the narrative of Colonel Smith, corroborated by other testimony.

The commander-in-chief had already heard of the accident that befell Pierce the day before; and as the latter approached, General Scott could not but notice the marks of pain and physical exhaustion, against which only the sturdiest constancy of will could have enabled him to bear up. "Pierce, my dear fellow," said he,—and that epithet of familiar kindness and friendship, upon the battle field, was the highest of military commendation from such a man,—"you are badly injured; you are not fit to be in your saddle." "Yes, general, I am," replied Pierce, "in a case like this." "You cannot touch your foot to the stirrup," said Scott. "One of them I can," answered Pierce. The general looked again at Pierce's almost disabled figure, and seemed on the point of taking his irrevocable resolution. "You are rash, General Pierce," said he; "we shall lose you, and we cannot spare you. It is my duty to order you back to St. Augustine." "For God's sake, general," exclaimed Pierce, "don't say that! This is the last great battle, and I must lead my brigade!" The commander-in-chief made no further remonstrance, but gave the order for Pierce to advance with his brigade.

The way lay through thick standing corn, and over marshy ground intersected with ditches, which were filled, or partially so, with water. Over some of the narrower of these Pierce leaped his horse. When the brigade had advanced about a mile, however, it found itself impeded by a ditch ten or twelve feet wide, and six or eight feet deep. It being impossible to leap it, General Pierce was lifted from his saddle, and, in some incomprehensible way, hurt as he was, contrived to wade or scramble across this obstacle, leaving his horse on the hither side. The troops were now under fire. In the excitement of the battle, he forgot his injury, and hurried forward, leading the brigade, a distance of two or three hundred yards. But the exhaustion of his frame, and particularly the anguish of his knee,—made more intolerable by such free use of it,—was greater than any strength of nerve, or any degree of mental energy, could struggle against. He fell, faint and almost insensible, within full range of the enemy's fire. It was proposed to bear him off the field; but, as some of his soldiers approached to lift him, be became aware of their purpose, and was partially revived by his determination to resist it. "No," said he, with all the strength he had left, "don't carry me off! Let me lie here!" And there he lay, under the tremendous fire of Churubusco, until the enemy, in total rout, was driven from the field.

Immediately after the victory, when the city of Mexico lay at the mercy of the American commander, and might have been entered that very night, Santa Anna sent a flag of truce, proposing an armistice, with a view to negotiations for peace. It cannot be considered in any other light than as a very high and signal compliment to his gallantry in the field, that General Pierce was appointed, by the commander-in-chief, one of the commissioners on our part, together with General Quitman and General Persifer F. Smith, to arrange the terms of this armistice. Pierce was unable to walk, or to mount his horse without assistance, when intelligence of his appointment reached him. He had not taken off his spurs, nor slept an hour, for two nights; but he immediately obeyed the summons, was assisted into the saddle, and rode to Tacubaya, where, at the house of the British consul general, the American and Mexican commissioners were assembled. The conference began late in the afternoon, and continued till four o'clock the next morning, when the articles were signed. Pierce then proceeded to the quarters of General Worth, in the village of Tacubaya, where he obtained an hour or two of repose.

The expectation of General Scott, that further bloodshed might be avoided by means of the armistice, proved deceptive. Military operations, after a temporary interruption, were actively renewed; and on the 8th of September was fought the bloody battle of Molino del Rey, one of the fiercest and most destructive of the war.

In this conflict General Worth, with three thousand troops, attacked and routed fourteen thousand Mexicans, driving them under the protection of the Castle of Chepultepec. Perceiving the obstinacy with which the field was contested, the commander-in-chief despatched an order to General Pierce to advance to the support of General Worth's division. He moved forward with rapidity; and although the battle was won just as he reached the field, he interposed his brigade between Worth and the retreating enemy, and thus drew upon himself the fire of Chepultepec. A shell came streaming from the castle, and, bursting within a few feet of him, startled his horse, which was near plunging over an adjacent precipice. Continuing a long time under fire, Pierce's brigade was engaged in removing the wounded, and the captured ammunition. While thus occupied, he led a portion of his command to repel the attacks of the enemy's skirmishers.

There remained but one other battle,—that of Chepultepec,— which was fought on the 13th of September. On the preceding day, (although the injuries and the over-exertion, resulting from previous marches and battles, had greatly enfeebled him,) General Pierce had acted with his brigade. In obedience to orders, it had occupied the field of Molino del Rey. Contrary to expectation, it was found that the enemy's force had been withdrawn from this position. Pierce remained in the field until noon, when, it being certain that the anticipated attack would not take place before the following day, he returned to the quarters of General Worth, which were near at hand. There he became extremely ill, and was unable to leave his bed for the thirty-six hours next ensuing. In the mean time, the Castle of Chepultepec was stormed by the troops under Generals Pillow and Quitman. Pierce's brigade behaved itself gallantly, and suffered severely; and that accomplished officer, Colonel Ransom, leading the Ninth Regiment to the attack, was shot through the head, and fell, with many other brave men, in that last battle of the war.

The American troops, under Quitman and Worth, had established themselves within the limits of the city, having possession of the gates of Belen and of San Cosma, but, up till nightfall, had met with a vigorous resistance from the Mexicans, led on by Santa Anna in person. They had still, apparently, a desperate task before them. It was anticipated, that, with the next morning's light, our troops would be ordered to storm the citadel, and the city of Mexico itself. When this was told to Pierce, upon his sick bed, he rose, and attempted to dress himself; but Captain Hardcastle, who had brought the intelligence from Worth, prevailed upon him to remain in bed, and not to exhaust his scanty strength, until the imminence of the occasion should require his presence. Pierce acquiesced for the time, but again arose, in the course of the night, and made his way to the trenches, where he reported himself to General Quitman, with whose division was a part of his brigade. Quitman's share in the anticipated assault, it was supposed, owing to the position which his troops occupied, would be more perilous than that of Worth.   But the last great battle had been fought. In the morning, it was discovered that the citadel had been abandoned, and that Santa Anna had withdrawn his army from the city.

There never was a more gallant body of officers than those who came from civil life into the army on occasion of the Mexican war. All of them, from the rank of general downward, appear to have been animated by the spirit of young knights, in times of chivalry, when fighting for their spurs. Hitherto known only as peaceful citizens, they felt it incumbent on them, by daring and desperate valor, to prove their fitness to be intrusted with the guardianship of their country's honor. The old and trained soldier, already distinguished on former fields, was free to be discreet as well as brave; but these untried warriors were in a different position, and therefore rushed on perils with reckless- ness that found its penalty on every battle field—not one of which was won without a grievous sacrifice of the best blood of America. In this band of gallant men, it is not too much to say, General Pierce was as distinguished for what we must term his temerity in personal expo- sure, as the higher traits of leadership, wherever there was an oppor- tunity for their display.

He had manifested, moreover, other and better qualities than these, and such as it affords his biographer far greater pleasure to record. His tenderness of heart, his sympathy, his brotherly or pater- nal care for his men, had been displayed in a hundred instances, and had gained him the enthusiastic affection of all who served under his command. During the passage from America, under the tropics, he would go down into the stifling air of the hold, with a lemon, a cup of tea, and, better and more efficacious than all, a kind word, for the sick. While encamped before Vera Cruz, he gave up his own tent to a sick comrade, and went himself to lodge in the pestilential city. On the march, and even on the battle field, he found occasion to exercise those feelings of humanity which show most beautifully there. And, in the hospitals of Mexico, he went among the diseased and wounded soldiers, cheering them with his voice and the magic of his kindness, inquiring into their wants, and relieving them to the utmost of his pecuniary means. There was not a man of his brigade but loved him, and would have followed him to death, or have sacrificed his own life in his general's defence.

The officers of the old army, whose profession was war, and who well knew what a soldier was, and ought to be, fully recognized his merit. An instance of their honorable testimony in his behalf may fitly be recorded here. It was after General Pierce had returned to the United States. At a dinner in the Halls of Montezuma, at which forty or fifty of the brave men above alluded to were present, a young officer of the New England regiment was called on for a toast. He made an address, in which he spoke with irrepressible enthusiasm of General Pierce, and begged to propose his health. One of the officers of the old line rose, and observed, that none of the recently appointed generals commanded more unanimous and universal respect; that General Pierce had appreciated the scientific knowledge of the regular military men, and had acquired their respect by the independence, firmness, and promptitude, with which he exercised his own judgment, and acted on the intelligence derived from them. In concluding this tribute of high, but well-considered praise, the speaker very cordially acquiesced in the health of General Pierce, and proposed that it should be drunk standing, with three times three.

General Pierce remained in Mexico until December, when, as the warfare was over, and peace on the point of being concluded, be set out on his return. In nine months, crowded full of incident, he had seen far more of actual service, than many professional soldiers during their whole lives. As soon as the treaty of peace was signed, he gave up his commission, and returned to the practice of the law, again proposing to spend the remainder of his days in the bosom of his family. All the dreams of his youth were now fulfilled; the military ardor, that had struck an hereditary root in his breast, had enjoyed its scope, and was satisfied; and he flattered himself that no circumstances could hereafter occur to draw him from the retirement of domestic peace. New Hampshire received him with pride and honor, and with even more enthusiastic affection than ever. At his departure, he had received a splendid sword at the hands of many of his friends, in token of their confidence; he had shown himself well worthy to wear, and able to use, a soldier's weapon; and his native state now gave him another, the testimonial of approved valor and warlike conduct.

6

THE COMPROMISE AND OTHER MATTERS

THE INTERVENING YEARS, since General Pierce's return from Mexico, and until the present time, have been spent in the laborious exercise of the legal profession—an employment scarcely varied or interrupted, except by those episodes of political activity which a man of public influence finds it impossible to avoid, and in which, if his opinions are matter of conscience with him, he feels it his duty to interest himself.

In the presidential canvass of 1848 he used his best efforts (and with success, so far as New Hampshire was concerned) in behalf of the candidate of his party. A truer and better speech has never been uttered, on a similar occasion, than one which he made, (during a hurried half hour, snatched from the court room,) in October of the above year, before the democratic state convention, then in session at Concord. It is an invariable characteristic of General Pierce's popular addresses, that they evince a genuine respect for the people; he makes his appeal to their intelligence, their patriotism, and their integrity, and, never doubtful of their upright purpose, proves his faith in the great mind and heart of the country both by what he says and by what he refrains from saying. He never yet was guilty of an effort to cajole his fellow-citizens, to operate upon their credulity, or to trick them even into what was right; and therefore all the victories which he has ever won in popular assemblies have been triumphs doubly honored, being as creditable to his audiences as to himself.

When the series of measures known under the collective term of The Compromise were passed by Congress, in 1850, and put to so searching a test, here at the north, the reverence of the people for the constitution, and their attachment to the Union, General Pierce was true to the principles which he had long ago avowed. At an early period of his congressional service, he had made known, with the perfect frankness of his character, those opinions upon the slavery question which he has never since seen occasion to change in the slightest degree. There is an unbroken consistency in his action with regard to this matter. It is entirely of a piece, from his first entrance upon public life until the moment when he came forward, while many were faltering, to throw the great weight of his character and influence into the scale in favor of those measures through which it was intended to redeem the pledges of the constitution, and to preserve and renew the old love and harmony among the sisterhood of states. His approval embraced the whole series of these acts, as well those which bore hard upon northern views and sentiments as those in which the south deemed itself to have made more than reciprocal concessions.

No friend nor enemy, that knew Franklin Pierce, would have expected him to act otherwise. With his view of the whole subject, whether looking at it through the medium of his conscience, his feelings, or his intellect, it was impossible for him not to take his stand as the unshaken advocate of Union, and of the mutual steps of compromise which that great object unquestionably demanded. The fiercest, the least scrupulous, and the most consistent of those who battle against slavery recognize the same fact that he does. They see that merely human wisdom and human efforts cannot subvert it except by tearing to pieces the constitution, breaking the pledges which it sanctions, and severing into distracted fragments that common country which Providence brought into one nation, through a continued miracle of almost two hundred years, from the first settlement of the American wilderness until the revolution. In the days when, a young member of Congress, he first raised his voice against agitation, Pierce saw these perils and their consequences. He considered, too, that the evil would be certain, while the good was, at best, a contingency, and (to the clear, practical foresight with which he looked into the future) scarcely so much as that, attended, as the movement was and must be, during its progress, with the aggravated injury of those whose condition it aimed to ameliorate, and terminating, in its possible triumph,— if such possibility there were,—with the ruin of two races which now dwelt together in greater peace and affection, it is not too much to say, than had ever elsewhere existed between the taskmaster and the serf.

Of course, there is another view of all these matters. The theorist may take that view in his closet; the philanthropist by profession may strive to act upon it uncompromisingly, amid the tumult and warfare of his life. But the statesman of practical sagacity—who loves his country as it is, and evolves good from things as they exist, and who demands to feel his firm grasp upon a better reality before he quits the one already gained—will be likely here, with all the greatest statesmen of America, to stand in the attitude of a conservative. Such, at all events, will be the attitude of Franklin Pierce. We have sketched some of the influences amid which he grew up, inheriting his father's love of country, mindful of the old patriot's valor in so many conflicts of the revolution, and having close before his eyes the example of brothers and relatives, more than one of whom have bled for America, both at the extremest north and farthest south; himself, too, in early manhood, serving the Union in its legislative halls, and, at a maturer age, leading his fellow-citizens, his brethren, from the widest-sundered states, to redden the same battle fields with their kindred blood, to unite their breath in one shout of victory, and perhaps to sleep, side by side, with the same sod over them. Such a man, with such hereditary recollections, and such a personal experience, must not narrow himself to adopt the cause of one section of his native country against another. He will stand up, as he has always stood, among the patriots of the whole land. And if the work of anti-slavery agitation, which it is undeniable, leaves most men who earnestly engage in it with only half a country in their affections—if this work must be done, let others do it.

Those northern men, therefore, who deem the great cause of human welfare all represented and involved in this present hostility against southern institutions, and who conceive that the world stands still except so far as that goes forward—these, it may be allowed, can scarcely give their sympathy or their confidence to the subject of this memoir. But there is still another view, and probably as wise a one. It looks upon slavery as one of those evils which divine Providence does not leave to be remedied by human contrivances, but which, in its own good time, by some means impossible to be anticipated, but of the simplest and easiest operation, when all its uses shall have been fulfilled, it causes to vanish like a dream. There is no instance, in all history, of the human will and intellect having perfected any great moral reform by methods which it adapted to that end; but the progress of the world, at every step, leaves some evil or wrong on the path behind it, which the wisest of mankind, of their own set purpose, could never have found the way to rectify. Whatever contributes to the great cause of good, contributes to all its subdivisions and varieties; and, on this score, the lover of his race, the enthusiast, the philanthropist of whatever theory, might lend his aid to put a man, like the one before us, in the leadership of the world's affairs.

How firm and conscientious was General Pierce's support of the Compromise, may be estimated from his conduct in reference to the reverend John Atwood. In the foregoing pages it has come oftener in our way to illustrate the bland and prepossessing features of General Pierce's character, than those sterner ones which must necessarily form the bones, so to speak, the massive skeleton, of any man who retains an upright attitude amidst the sinister influences of public life. The transaction now alluded to affords a favorable opportunity for indicating some of these latter traits.

In October, 1850, a democratic convention, held at Concord, nominated Mr. Atwood as the party's regular candidate for governor. The Compromise, then recent, was inevitably a prominent element in the discussions of the convention; and a series of resolutions were adopted, bearing reference to this great subject, fully and unreservedly indorsing the measures comprehended under it, and declaring the principles on which the Democracy of the state was about to engage in the gubernatorial contest. Mr. Atwood accepted the nomination, acceding to the platform thus tendered him, takeing exceptions to none of the individual resolutions, and, of course, pledging himself to the whole by the very act of assuming the candidacy, which was predicated upon them.

The reverend candidate, we should conceive, is a well-meaning, and probably an amiable man. In ordinary circumstances, he would, doubtless, have gone through the canvass triumphantly, and have administered the high office to which he aspired with no discredit to the party that had placed him at its head. But the disturbed state of the public mind on the Compromise Question rendered the season a very critical one; and Mr. Atwood, unfortunately, had that fatal weakness of character, which, however respectably it may pass in quiet times, is always bound to make itself pitiably manifest under the pressure of a crisis. A letter was addressed to him by a committee, representing the party opposed to the Compromise, and with whom, it may be supposed, were included those who held the more thoroughgoing degrees of anti-slavery sentiment. The purpose of the letter was to draw out an expression of Mr. Atwood's opinion on the abolition movement generally, and with an especial reference to the Fugitive Slave Law, and whether, as chief magistrate of the state, he would favor any attempt for its repeal. In an answer of considerable length, the candidate expressed sentiments that brought him unquestionably within the Free Soil pale, and favored his correspondents, moreover, with a pretty decided judgment as to the unconstitutional, unjust, and oppressive character of the Fugitive Slave act.

During a space of about two months, this very important document was kept from the public eye. Rumors of its existence, however, became gradually noised abroad, and necessarily attracted the attention of Mr. Atwood's democratic friends. Inquiries being made, he acknowledged the existence of the letter, but averred that it had never been delivered, that it was merely a rough draught, and that he had hitherto kept it within his own control, with a view to more careful consideration. In accordance with the advice of friends, he expressed a determination, and apparently in good faith, to suppress the letter, and thus to sever all connection with the anti-slavery party. This, however, was now beyond his power. A copy of the letter had been taken; it was published, with high commendations, in the anti-slavery newspapers; and Mr. Atwood was exhibited in the awkward predicament of directly avowing sentiments on the one band which be had implicitly disavowed, on the other, of accepting a nomination based on principles diametrically opposite.

The candidate appears to have apprehended this disclosure, and he hurried to Concord, and sought counsel of General Pierce, with whom he was on terms of personal kindness, and between whom and himself, heretofore, there had never been a shade of political difference. An interview with the general and one or two other gentlemen ensued. Mr. Atwood was cautioned against saying or writing a word that might be repugnant to his feelings or his principles; but, voluntarily, and at his own suggestion, he now wrote, for publication, a second letter, in which he retracted every objectionable feature of his former one, and took decided ground in favor of the Compromise, including all its individual measures. Had he adhered to this latter position, he might have come out of the affair, if not with the credit of consistency, yet, at least, as a successful candidate in the impending election. But his evil fate, or, rather, the natural infirmity of his character, was not so to be thrown off. The very next day, unhappily, he fell into the hands of some of his anti-slavery friends, to whom he avowed a constant adherence to the principles of his first letter, describing the second as having been drawn from him by importunity, in an excited state of his mind, and without a full realization of its purport.

It would be needlessly cruel to Mr. Atwood to trace, with minuteness, the further details of this affair. It is impossible to withhold from him a certain sympathy, or to avoid feeling that a worthy man, as the world goes, had entangled himself in an inextricable knot of duplicity and tergiversation, by an ill-advised effort to be opposite things at once. For the sake of true manhood, we gladly turn to consider the course adopted by General Pierce.

The election for governor was now at a distance of only a few weeks; and it could not be otherwise than a most hazardous movement for the democratic party, at so late a period, to discard a candidate with whom the people had become familiar. It involved nothing less than the imminent peril of that political supremacy which the party had so long enjoyed. With Mr. Atwood as candidate, success might still be considered certain. To a short-sighted and a weak man, it would have appeared the obvious policy to patch up the difficulty, and, at all events, to conquer, under whatever leadership, and with whatever allies. But it was one of those junctures which test the difference between the man of principle and the mere politician—the man of moral courage and him who yields to temporary expediency. General Pierce could not consent that his party should gain a nominal triumph, at the expense of what looked upon as its real integrity and life. With this view this of the matter, he had no hesitation in his course; nor could the motives which otherwise would have been strongest with him—pity for the situation of an unfortunate individual, a personal friend, a democrat, as Mr. Atwood describes himself, of nearly fifty years' standing—incline him to mercy, where it would have been fatal to his sense of right. He took decided ground against Mr. Atwood. The convention met again, and nominated another candidate. Mr. Atwood went into the field as the candidate of the anti-slavery party, drew off a sufficient body of democrats to defeat the election by the people, but was himself defeated in the legislature.

Thus, after exhibiting to the eyes of mankind (or such portion of mankind as chanced to be looking in that direction) the absurd spectacle of a gentleman of extremely moderate stride attempting a feat that would have baffled a Colossus,—to support himself, namely, on both margins of the impassable chasm that has always divided the anti-slavery faction from the New Hampshire Democracy,—this ill-fated man attempted first to throw himself upon one side of the gulf, then on the other, and finally tumbled headlong into the bottomless depth between. His case presents a painful, but very curious and instructive instance of the troubles that beset weakness, in those emergencies which demand steadfast moral strength and energy—of which latter type of manly character there can be no truer example than Franklin Pierce.

In the autumn of 1850, in pursuance of a vote of the people, a convention assembled at Concord for the revision of the constitution of New Hampshire. General Pierce was elected its president by an almost unanimous vote—a very high mark of the affectionate confidence which the state, for so long a time, and in such a variety of modes, had manifested in him. It was so much the higher, as the convention included New Hampshire's most eminent citizens, among whom was Judge Woodbury.

General Pierce's conduct, as presiding officer, was satisfactory to all parties; and one of his political opponents (Professor Sanborn, of Dartmouth College) has ably sketched him, both in that aspect and as a debater.

"In drawing the portraits of the distinguished members of the constitutional convention," writes the professor, "to pass Frank Pierce unnoticed would be as absurd as to enact one of Shakspeare's dramas without its principal hero. I give my impressions of the man as I saw him in the convention; for I would not undertake to vouch for the truth or falsehood of those veracious organs of public sentiment, at the capital, which have loaded him, in turn, with indiscriminate praise and abuse. As a presiding officer, it would be difficult to find his equal. In proposing questions to the house, he never hesitates or blunders. In deciding points of order, he is both prompt and impartial. His treatment of every member of the convention was characterized by uniform courtesy and kindness. The deportment of the presiding officer of a deliberative body usually gives tone to the debates. If he is harsh, morose, or abrupt in his manner, the speakers are apt to catch his spirit by the force of involuntary sympathy. The same is true, to some extent, of the principal debaters in such a body. When a man of strong prejudices and harsh temper rises to address a public assembly, his indwelling antipathies speak from every feature of his face, and from every motion of his person. The audience at once brace themselves against his assaults, and condemn his opinions before they are heard. The well-known character of an orator persuades or dissuades quite as forcibly as the language he utters. Some men never rise to address a deliberative assembly without conciliating good will in advance. The smile that plays upon the speaker's face awakens emotions of complacency in those who hear, even before be speaks. So does that weight of character, which is the matured fruit of long public services and acknowledged worth, soothe, in advance, the irritated and angry crowd.

"Mr. Pierce possesses unquestioned ability as a public speaker. Few men, in our country, better understand the means of swaying a popular assembly, or employ them with greater success. His forte lies in moving the passions of those whom he addresses. He knows how to call into vigorous action both the sympathies and antipathies of those who listen to him. I do not mean to imply by these remarks that his oratory is deficient in argument or sound reasoning. On the contrary, he seizes with great power upon the strong points of his subject, and presents them clearly, forcibly, and eloquently. As a prompt and ready debater, always prepared for assault or defence, he has few equals. In these encounters, he appears to great advantage, from his happy faculty of turning little incidents, unexpectedly occurring, to his own account. A word carelessly dropped, or an unguarded allusion to individuals or parties, by an opponent, is frequently converted into a powerful weapon of assault, by this skilful advocate. He has been so much in office, that he may be said to have been educated in public life. He is most thoroughly versed in all the tactics of debate. He is not only remarkably fluent in his elocution, but remarkably correct. He seldom miscalls or repeats a word. His style is not overloaded with ornament, and yet he draws liberally upon the treasury of rhetoric. His figures are often beautiful and striking, never incongruous. He is always listened to with respectful attention, if he does not always command conviction. From his whole course in the convention, a disinterested spectator could not fail to form a very favorable opinion, not only of his talent and eloquence, but of his generosity and magnanimity."

Among other antiquated relics of the past and mouldy types of prejudices that ought now to be forgotten, and of which it was the object
of the present convention to purge the constitution of New
Hampshire, there is a provision, that certain state offices should be
held only by Protestants. Since General Pierce's nomination for the
presidency, the existence of this religious test has been brought as a
charge against him, as if, in spite of his continued efforts to remove it,
he were personally responsible for its remaining on the statute book.

General Pierce has naturally a strong endowment of religious
feeling. At no period of his life, as is well known to his friends, have
the sacred relations of the human soul been a matter of indifference
with him; and, of more recent years, whatever circumstances of good
or evil fortune may have befallen him, they have alike served to
deepen this powerful sentiment. Whether in sorrow or success, he has
learned, in his own behalf, the great lesson, that religious faith is the
most valuable and most sacred of human possessions; but, with this
sense, there has come no narrowness or illiberality, but a wide-
embracing sympathy for the modes of Christian worship, and a reverence for individual belief, as a matter between the Deity and man's
soul, and with which no other has a right to interfere. With the feeling here described, and with his acute intellectual perception of the
abortive character of all intolerant measures, as defeating their own
ends, it strikes one as nothing less than ludicrous that he should be
charged with desiring to retain this obsolete enactment, standing, as
it does, as a merely gratuitous and otherwise inoperative stigma upon
the fair reputation of his native state. Even supposing no higher
motives to have influenced him, it would have sufficed to secure his
best efforts for the repeal of the religious test, that so many of the
Catholics have always been found in the advance-guard of freedom,
marching onward with the progressive party; and that, whether in
peace or war, they have performed their adopted country the hard toil
and the gallant services which she has a right to expect from her most
faithful citizens.

The truth is, that, ever since his entrance upon public life, on all
occasions,—and often making the occasion where he found none,—

General Pierce has done his utmost to obliterate this obnoxious feature from the constitution. He has repeatedly advocated the calling of a convention mainly for this purpose. In that of 1850, he both spoke and voted in favor of the abolition of the test, and, with the aid of Judge Woodbury and other democratic members, attained his purpose, so far as the convention possessed any power or responsibility in the matter. That the measure was ultimately defeated is due to other causes, either temporary or of long continuance; and to some of them it is attributable that the enlightened public sentiment of New Hampshire was not, long since, made to operate upon this enactment, so anomalous in the fundamental law of a free state.

In order to the validity of the amendments passed by the convention, it was necessary that the people should subsequently act upon them, and pass a vote of two thirds in favor of their adoption. The amendments proposed by the convention of 1850 were numerous. The constitution had been modified in many and very important particulars, in respect to which the popular mind had not previously been made familiar, and on which it had not anticipated the necessity of passing judgment. In March, 1851, when the vote of the people was taken upon these measures, the Atwood controversy was at its height, and threw all matters of less immediate interest into the background. During the interval since the adjournment of the convention, the whig newspapers had been indefatigable in their attempts to put its proceedings in an odious light before the people. There had been no period, for many years, in which sinister influences rendered it so difficult to draw out an efficient expression of the will of the democracy, as on this occasion. It was the result of all these obstacles, that the doings of the constitutional convention were rejected in the mass.

In the ensuing April, the convention reassembled, in order to receive the unfavorable verdict of the people upon its proposed amendments. At the suggestion of General Pierce, the amendment abolishing the religious test was again brought forward, and, in spite of the opposition of the leading whig members, was a second time submitted to the people. Nor did his struggle in behalf of this enlightened movement terminate here. At the democratic caucus, in

Concord, preliminary to the town meeting, he urged upon his political friends the repeal of the test, as a party measure; and again, at the town meeting itself, while the balloting was going forward, he advocated it on the higher ground of religious freedom, and of reverence for what is inviolable in the human soul. Had the amendment passed, the credit would have belonged to no man more than to General Pierce; and that it failed, and that the free constitution of New Hampshire is still disgraced by a provision which even monarchical England has cast off, is a responsibility which must rest elsewhere than on his head.

In September, 1851, died that eminent statesman and jurist, Levi Woodbury, then occupying the elevated post of judge of the Supreme Court of the United States. The connection between him and General Pierce, beginning in the early youth of the latter, had been sustained through all the subsequent years. They sat together, with but one intervening chair between, in the national Senate; they were always advocates of the same great measures, and held, through life, a harmony of opinion and action, which was never more conspicuous than in the few months that preceded Judge Woodbury's death. At a meeting of the bar, after his decease, General Pierce uttered some remarks, full of sensibility, in which he referred to the circumstances that had made this friendship an inheritance on his part. Had Judge Woodbury survived, it is not improbable that his more advanced age, his great public services, and equally distinguished zeal in behalf of the Union, might have placed him in the position now occupied by the subject of this memoir. Fortunate the state, which, after losing such a son, can still point to another, not less worthy to take upon him the charge of the nation's welfare.

We have now finished our record of Franklin Pierce's life, and have only to describe the posture of affairs which—without his own purpose, and against his wish—has placed him before the people of the United States, as a candidate for the presidency.

7

HIS NOMINATION FOR THE PRESIDENCY

ON THE 12TH OF JUNE, 1852, the democratic national convention assembled at Baltimore, in order to Select a candidate for the presidency of the United States. Many names, eminently distinguished in peace and war, had been brought before the public, during several months previous; and among them, though by no means occupying a very prominent place, was the name of Franklin Pierce. In January of this year, the democracy of New Hampshire had signified its preference of General Pierce as a presidential candidate in the approaching canvass—a demonstration which drew from him the following response, addressed to his friend, Mr. Atherton:—

> "I am far from being insensible to the generous confidence, so often manifested towards me by the people of this state; and although the object indicated in the resolution, having particular reference to myself, be not one of desire on my part, the expression is not on that account less gratifying.
> "Doubtless the spontaneous and just appreciation of an intelligent people is the best earthly reward for earnest and cheerful services rendered to one's state and country; and while it is a matter of unfeigned regret that my life has been so barren of usefulness, I shall ever hold this and similar tributes among my most cherished recollections.
> "To these, my sincere and grateful acknowledgments, I

desire to add, that the same motives which induced me, several years ago to retire from public life, and which, since that
time, controlled my judgment in this respect, now impel me
to say, that the use of my name, in any event, before the democratic national convention at Baltimore, to which you are a
delegate, would be utterly repugnant to my tastes and wishes."

The sentiments expressed in the above letter were genuine, and from
his heart. He had looked long and closely at the effects of high public
station on the character and happiness, and on what is the innermost
and dearest part of a man's possessions—his independence; and he
had satisfied himself that office, however elevated, should be avoided
for one's own sake, or accepted only as a good citizen would make any
other sacrifice, at the call and at the need of his country.

As the time for the assembling of the national convention drew
near, there were other sufficient indications of his sincerity in declining
a stake in the great game. A circular letter was addressed, by Major Scott
of Virginia, to the distinguished democrats whose claims had heretofore been publicly discussed, requesting a statement of their opinions
on several points, and inquiring what would be the course of each of
these gentlemen, in certain contingencies, in case of his attaining the
presidency. These queries, it may be presumed, were of such a nature
that General Pierce might have answered them, had he seen fit to do so,
to the satisfaction of Major Scott himself, or to that of the southern
democratic party, whom it seemed his purpose to represent. With not
more than one exception, the other statesmen and soldiers, to whom
the circular bad been sent, made a response. General Pierce preserved
an unbroken silence. It was equivalent to the withdrawal of all claims
which he might be supposed to possess, in reference to the contemplated office; and he thereby repeated, to the delegates of the national
party, the same avowal of distaste for public life which had already
made known to the Democracy of his native state. He had thus done
every thing in his power, actively or passively,—every thing that he
could have done, without showing such an estimate of his position
before the country as was inconsistent with the modesty of his charac-

ter,—to avoid the perilous and burdensome honor of the candidacy.

The convention met, at the date above mentioned, and continued its sessions during four days. Thirty-five ballotings were held, with a continually decreasing prospect that the friends of any one of the gentlemen hitherto prominent before the people would succeed in obtaining the two thirds vote that was requisite for a nomination. Thus far, not a vote had been thrown for General Pierce; but, at the thirty-sixth ballot, the delegation of old Virginia brought forward his name. In the course of several more trials, his strength increased, very gradually at first, but afterwards with a growing impetus, until, at the forty-ninth ballot, the votes were for Franklin Pierce two hundred and eighty-two, and eleven for all other candidates. Thus Franklin Pierce became the nominee of the convention; and as quickly as tile lightning flash could blazen it abroad, his name was on every tongue, from end to end of this vast country. Within an hour he grew to be illustrious.

It would be a pretension, which we do not mean to put forward, to assert that, whether considering the length and amount of his public services, or his prominence before the country, General Pierce stood on equal ground with several of the distinguished men, whose claims, to use the customary phrase, had been rejected in favor of his own. But no man, be his public services or sacrifices what they might, ever did or ever could possess, in the slightest degree, what we may term a legitimate claim to be elevated to the rulership of a free people. The nation would degrade itself, and violate every principle upon which its institutions are founded, by offering its majestic obedience to one of its citizens as a reward for whatever splendor of achievement. The conqueror may assert a claim such as it is, to the sovereignty of the people whom he subjugates; but, with us Americans, when a statesman comes to the chief direction of affairs, it is at the summons of the nation, addressed to the servant whom it deems best fitted to spend his wisdom, his strength, and his life, in its behalf. On this principle, which is obviously the correct one, a candidate's previous services are entitled to consideration only as they indicate the qualities which may enable him to render higher services in the position which his countrymen choose that be shall occupy. What he has done is of no importance, except as proving what he can do. And it is on this score, because they see in his public course the irrefragable evidences of patriotism, integrity, and courage, and because they recognize in him the noble gift of natural authority, and have a prescience of the stately endowment of administrative genius, that his fellow-citizens are about to summon Franklin Pierce to the presidency. To those who know him well, the event comes, not like accident, but as a consummation which might have been anticipated, from its innate fitness, and as the final step of a career which, all along, has tended thitherward.

It is not as a reward that be will take upon him the mighty burden of this office, of which the toil and awful responsibility whiten the statesman's head, and in which, as in more than one instance we have seen, the warrior encounters a deadlier risk than in the battle field. When General Pierce received the news of his nomination, it affected him with no thrill of joy, but a sadness, which, for many days, was perceptible in his deportment. It awoke in his heart the sense of religious dependence—a sentiment that has been growing continually stronger, through all the trials and experiences of his life; and there was nothing feigned in that passage of his beautiful letter, accepting the nomination, in which he expresses his reliance upon heavenly support.

The committee, appointed by the Baltimore convention, conveyed to him the intelligence of his nomination in the following terms:—

> "A national convention of the democratic republican party, which met in Baltimore on the first Tuesday in June, unanimously nominated you as a candidate for the high trust of the President of the United States. We have been delegated to acquaint you with the nomination, and earnestly to request that you will accept it. Persuaded as we are that this office should never be pursued by an unchastened ambition, it cannot be refused by a dutiful patriotism.   "The circumstances under which you will be presented for the canvass of your countrymen seem to us propitious to the interests which the

constitution intrusts to our Federal Union, and must be auspicious to your own name. You come before the people without the impulse of personal wishes, and free from selfish
expectations. You are identified with none of the distractions
which have recently disturbed our country, whilst you are
known to be faithful to the constitution—to all its guaranties
and compromises. You will be free to exercise your tried abilities, within the path of duty, in protecting that repose we
happily enjoy, and in giving efficacy and control to those car-
dinal principles that have already illustrated the party which
has now selected you as its leader—principles that regard the
security and prosperity of the whole country, and the paramount power of its laws, as indissolubly associated with the
perpetuity of our civil and religious liberties.

"The convention did not pretermit the duty of reiterating
those principles, and you will find them prominently set forth
in the resolutions it adopted. To these we respectfully invite
your attention. "It is firmly believed that to your talents and
patriotism the security of our holy Union, with its expanded
and expanding interests, may be wisely trusted, and that,
amid all the perils which may assail the constitution, you will
have the heart to love and the arm to defend it."

We quote likewise General Pierce's reply:—

"I have the honor to acknowledge your personal kindness in
presenting me, this day, your letter, officially informing me of
my nomination, by the democratic national convention, as a
candidate for the presidency of the United States. The surprise with which I received the intelligence of my nomination
was not unmingled with painful solicitude; and yet it is
proper for me to say that the manner in which it was con-
ferred was peculiarly gratifying.

The delegation from New Hampshire, with all the glow
of state pride, and with all the warmth of personal regard,

would not have submitted my name to the convention, nor would they have cast a vote for me, under circumstances other than those which occurred.

"I shall always cherish with pride and gratitude the recollection of the fact, that the voice which first pronounced, and pronounced alone, came from the Mother of States—a pride and gratitude rising above any consequences that can betide me personally. May I not regard it as a fact pointing to the overthrow of sectional jealousies, and looking to the permanent life and vigor of the Union, cemented by the blood of those who have passed to their reward?—a Union wonderful in its formation, boundless in its hopes, amazing in its destiny.

"I accept the nomination, relying upon an abiding devotion to the interests, honor, and glory of the whole country, but, above and beyond all, upon a Power superior to all human might—a Power which, from the first gun of the revolution, in every crisis through which we have passed, in every hour of acknowledged peril, when the dark clouds had shut down over us, has interposed as if to baffle human wisdom, outmarch human forecast, and bring out of darkness the rainbow of promise. Weak myself, faith and hope repose there in security.

"I accept the nomination upon the platform adopted by the convention, not because this is expected of me as a candidate, but because the principles it embraces command the approbation of my judgment; and with them, I believe I can safely say, there has been no word nor act of my life in conflict."

The news of his nomination went abroad over the Union, and, far and wide, there came a response, in which was distinguishable a truer appreciation of some of General Pierce's leading traits than could have been anticipated, considering the unobtrusive tenor of his legislative life, and the lapse of time since he had entirely withdrawn himself from the nation's eye. It was the marvellous and mystic influence of character, in regard to which the judgment of the people is so seldom found erroneous, and which conveys the perception of itself through some medium higher and deeper than the intellect. Every where the country knows that a man of steadfast will, true heart, and generous qualities has been brought forward, to receive the suffrages of his fellow-citizens.

He comes before the people of the United States at a remarkable era in the history of this country and of the world. The two great parties of the nation appear—at least to an observer somewhat removed from both—to have nearly merged into one another; for they preserve the attitude of political antagonism rather through the effect of their old organizations, than because any great and radical principles are at present in dispute between them. The measures advocated by the one party, and resisted by the other, through a long series of years, have now ceased to be the pivots on which the election turns. The prominent statesmen, so long identified with those measures, will henceforth relinquish their controlling influence over public affairs. Both parties, it may likewise be said, are united in one common purpose— that of preserving our sacred Union, as the immovable basis from which the destinies, not of America alone, but of mankind at large, may be carried upward and consummated. And thus men stand together, in unwonted quiet and harmony, awaiting the new movement in advance which all these tokens indicate.

It remains for the citizens of this great country to decide, within the next few weeks, whether they will retard the steps of human progress by placing at its head an illustrious soldier, indeed, a patriot and one indelibly stamped into the history of the past, but who has already done his work, and has not in him the spirit of the present or of the coming time,—or whether they will put their trust in a new man, whom a life of energy and various activity has tested, but not worn out, and advance with him into the auspicious epoch upon which we are about to enter.

NOTES

A.

WE HAVE DONE far less than justice to Franklin Pierce's college standing, in our statement on page 6 Some circumstances connected with this matter are too characteristic not to be recorded.

During the first two years, Pierce was extremely inattentive to his college duties, bestowing only such modicum of time upon them as was requisite to supply the merest superficial acquaintance with the course of study, for the recitation room. The consequence was, that, when the relative standing of the members of the class was first authoritatively ascertained, in the junior year, he found himself occupying precisely the lowest position in point of scholarship. In the first mortification of wounded pride, he resolved never to attend another recitation, and accordingly absented himself from college exercises of all kinds for several days, expecting and desiring that some form of punishment, such as suspension or expulsion, would be the result. The faculty of the college, however, with a wise lenity, took no notice of this behavior; and at last, having had time to grow cool, and moved by the grief of his friend Little and another classmate, Pierce determined to resume the routine of college duties. "But," said he to his friends, "if I do so, you shall see a change!"

Accordingly, from that time forward, he devoted himself to study. His mind, having run wild for so long a period, could be reclaimed only by the severest efforts of an iron resolution; and for three months afterwards, be rose at four in the morning, toiled all day over his books, and retired only at midnight, allowing himself but four hours for sleep. With habit and exercise, he acquired command over his intellectual powers, and was no longer under the necessity of application so intense. But from the moment when he made his resolve until the close of his college life, he never incurred a censure, never was absent (and then unavoidably) but from two college exercises, never went into the recitation room without a thorough acquaintance with the subject to be recited, and finally graduated as the third scholar of his class. Nothing save the low standard of his previous scholarship prevented his taking a yet higher rank.

The moral of this little story lies in the stern and continued exercise of self-controlling will, which redeemed him from indolence, completely changed the aspect of his character, and made this the

B.

IN THE DEARTH of other matter with which to carry on the war, the whig journals lay great stress on the responsibility which they allege against General Pierce and his political friends for the continued existence of the religious test in the constitution of New Hampshire. Since our own remarks on this subject were in type, we have examined a pamphlet, from the press of the *Boston Post*, in which the question is thoroughly discussed, and facts adduced which irrefragably prove the following positions, viz.:—

> "That the exclusion clauses in the New Hampshire constitution were put into it in 1784, before parties had formed, and were retained in it in 1792, when the federal or whig party was in power; and that to expunge them, it requires that a convention be called, and that a vote of two thirds of the people should accept the amendments it proposes, while it is made a duty of the people to vote on the question of calling a convention every seven years:
>
> "That the democratic journals have denounced these exclusion clauses as contrary to every principle of reason, jus-

tice, and common sense, and constantly advocated a revision of the constitution:

"That the leading democratic politicians have taken the same course in their political speeches; and instances are specified where they have, in political meetings, gone from town to town advocating a convention:

"That democratic county and state conventions have, in formal resolutions, unqualifiedly repudiated these clauses, and declared in favor of a revision of the constitution; and these resolutions are quoted:

"That so united was thought to be democratic public opinion against them, and so thoroughly was it in favor of a revision of the constitution, that its leading organ, the N. H. Patriot, October 17, 1844, declared that the universal sense of the democratic party was against them, and asserted, October 31, 1844, that it could say, with truth, there was not one intelligent member of the democratic party who was not in favor of a revision of the constitution:

"That in the convention of 1850, called to revise the constitution, Judge Woodbury and General Pierce made speeches against this test; and in a second session, after the amendments had been rejected, that they succeeded in getting the question submitted, together with another question, to the people: "That in all these movements General Pierce actively participated: that in the canvass of 1844, he went from town to town urging a revision of the constitution, and that year was denounced by the whigs because he advised all the democratic votes to be printed in favor of a call for a convention: that in 1845, he, with others, in a democratic convention, reported a resolution, which passed, repudiating the tests: that in 1850, he labored in the convention, in both sessions, to repeal it: that in the caucus of the democrats at Concord, and in town meeting in Concord, he made speeches in favor of blotting out the test that he has uniformly, by pen and speech, denounced it as a stigma on the state:

"That the whig assertion, that the democratic party could every seven years have repealed this test 'for the last sixty years' or 'at any time the last quarter of a century,' is a enormous falsehood; for facts show that it was not until the sixth septennial period, or 1829, that the democrats obtained even a majority ascendancy: that within twenty-five years there have been two whig governors, that in 1838 their majority was but 2800, in 1843 but 1600, and in 1846 they were in a minority, and that, in a contest, they never have had the two thirds vote required to alter the constitution: and that, at the only period when amendments to the constitution have been voted on since 1792, that is, on the amendments of 1850, the democratic party lacked ten thousand votes of having two thirds:

"That whig editorials, during the canvass of 1844, previous to the convention of 1850, during the sittings of the first session of that convention, and at its second session,—all which are quoted, and the dates of which are given,—either were in opposition to the call of a convention, or threatened that, if amendments approved by them were not adopted, opposition would be made to all amendment, or endeavored to array the prejudice of the people against the convention and its amendments, on the ground that of its forty thousand dollars expense, and, forsooth, because the convention chose to pass a series of compromise resolutions introduced by General Pierce. There is the language of the whig editorials, and it speaks for itself. All this shows conclusively that while the democratic party, in a the various ways it could, was denouncing the tests and urging a convention, the whig party was endeavoring to turn democratic action to party account. There is the record, and its force cannot be avoided. The inference is a just and a fair one—had the whig organs forgot party, the tests would have been abolished!

"Such is the conclusiveness with which the democratic party and General Pierce can be vindicated from this charge of intolerance, and such is the position of the party that makes this charge! But, setting all this aside, is it too much to invoke the candid and the patriotic, of all parties, to brand this business as disgraceful to those who engage in it; and to denounce this special appeal to a sect in religion, in order to get its members to vote a certain way in politics, as a gross violation of the spirit of our institutions, and a wanton insult alike to the intelligence and patriotism of American citizens? This desperate and unparalleled electioneering experiment, for ma

> "Again we ask, As truth makes its way in the track of falsehood, will not the base charge, instead of injuring General Pierce or the democratic party, recoil with fearful effect on those who utter it?"

At the town meeting in Concord, while the votes were being cast on the amendments proposed by the constitutional convention, General Pierce addressed his fellow-citizens with reference to the test. His speech is described as one which, for impassioned eloquence and power, could scarcely be surpassed; and it is difficult to imagine a stronger expression of abhorrence for the obnoxious law than is contained in the following imperfectly- reported passage:—

> "Can it be possible," said he, "that the people of New Hampshire will vote to retain a feature in its fundamental law, ingrafted there under peculiar circumstances, repugnant to the plainest ideas of justice and equality, repugnant to the whole scope and tenor of the constitution, upon which it stands as a fungus—dead, to be sure, but still there, a blot and deformity, obnoxious in the last degree to the spirit of the age in which we live? How can we say that our land is the asylum of th oppressed of other countries, when we fail to extend over them the shield of equal rights, and say to them, There is the panoply under which, so far as the dearest and most sacred of all rights is concerned, you may shelter yourselves? I love and revere the faith of my Protestant fathers; but do not Martin Lawler and his countrymen, now near me, and who

have this day exercised the rights of freemen, revere and cling to the faith of their fathers? Are you to tell them that they can vote for you, but are to be excluded from the privilege of being voted for? that while you tax them to maintain your government, they shall not be eligible to positions that control taxation ? Shame upon such a provision, while we boast of equal rights! I hope this provision of our constitution receives the deliberate reprobation of every man now in this hall. But if I am mistaken in this, it is due to the honor of the state, it is due to the plainest dictates of justice, that whoever may favor this test should state the reasons upon which he relies. For one, I never think of it without a deep sense of regret, and, I may add, of humiliation for my native state."

THE END.

INDEX

DATE DUE